COCKTAILS
INTERNATIONAL

COCKTAILS

INTERNATIONAL

Cocktail recipes from around the world
by MICHAEL WALKER

Published in association
with De Kuyper
Liqueurs

WILLOW BOOKS
Collins
8 Grafton Street, London
1983

CONTENTS

Introduction	6
Glossary	10
BEFORE YOU BEGIN	12
Stocking Up	14
Equipment	18
Glasses	24
Garnishes	28
Methods and Serving	32
RECIPES	38
Classic Cocktails	40
Spirit Cocktails	44
Cocktails with Fruit	58
Cream Cocktails	68
Wine Cocktails and Punches	74
Champagne Cocktails	80
Non-Alcoholic Cocktails	88
The Morning After	93
Index	95
Acknowledgements	96

Willow Books
William Collins Sons & Co Ltd
London . Glasgow . Sydney
Auckland . Toronto . Johannesburg

First published in Great Britain 1983
© William Collins Sons & Co Ltd 1983

Directed and edited for Willow Books
by Rosalie Vicars-Harris, New Media
Publishing Ltd

Photography by Robert Golden

Design and art direction by Rick Fawcett/Dark
Design Studio

Walker, Michael, 1947-
The cocktail book
1. cocktails
641.8'74   TX951

ISBN 0 00 218044 8

Filmset by SX Composing, Rayleigh, Essex

Printed in Italy by New Interlitho S.P.A.

INTRODUCTION

Cocktails have now become so popular internationally, to be drunk both in the home and in the many new cocktail bars that have opened up, that here we reflect on the cocktail story and take a look at some very different cocktail bars around the world, chosen for their professionalism, individuality and inventiveness.

The Golden Age of cocktails was the 'Roaring Twenties', when a cocktail was simply a drink of three or four ingredients mixed together by being shaken or stirred. It is interesting to reflect that cocktails reached a peak of popularity during the economic recession of the 1920s, and that there has been a noticeable revival of interest in cocktails worldwide at a time of yet another major economic recession in the 1980s. This is illustrated by the wave of new cocktail bars opening all over the world. Even more significantly, this new awakened fashion has brought cocktails into the home to a degree unprecedented even in the 1920s. Perhaps it is the fantasy element of these drinks that make them particularly popular at a time when people want to escape the realities of a depression, even though the cocktail's flamboyant character also makes it perfect for celebration. A more important influence perhaps is the current easy availability of equipment and the amazing range of spirits, liqueurs and exotic fruit juices from all over the world, which has led to the creation of a 'new wave' in the world of cocktails.

Along with the invention of the new and exotic types of cocktails has emerged the new style cocktail barman. It is regrettable that in many countries there is not the opportunity for many would-be barmen to have a thorough and professional training, with the result that there are extreme and sometimes disappointing variations of some of the more universally popular concoctions. Not only the face and the attitude of the barmen

The Oblomow Cocktail Bar is a small bar which serves only cocktails and is situated above the very friendly and popular Oblomow pub in Amsterdam's famous Reguliersdwarstraat. The décor of the bar is in the mood of the 1920s with a predominantly black and white theme. The copper bar, with its highly polished effect gives the illusion that your drinks are resting on a mirror. Although there are many bars in Amsterdam, this particular bar has attained a certain ambiance which has made it one of Amsterdam's most popular. From Oblomow come two great favourites with many of their customers:

Ramos Fizz *(far right)*
This cocktail has properties which will help resurrect 'the morning after'.
1 measure gin
2 measures orange juice
2 measures double cream
¼ measure gomme syrup
2 egg whites
2 drops orange flower water
Place all the ingredients into a blender with four or five cubes of ice and blend until smooth. Pour into a tall highball glass and decorate with a slice of orange and a cherry speared onto a cocktail stick. Add a thick straw through which the cocktail should be sipped.

Krakatao *(right)*
1 measure Kahlua
1 measure white crème de cacao
1 measure cream
1 dash Amaretto
Shake all the ingredients with ice. Strain into a cocktail glass decorated with a wedge of pineapple and a cherry.

Sardi's of New York is situated on West 44th Street and is run by the second generation of the Sardi family. This famous restaurant with its popular cocktail bar has been open for over 60 years and presents an image and a product that, although changing with the times, never vary in the qualities of excellence and elegance. The largely theatrical clientèle comprises of not only the companies of the various Broadway productions playing, but their audiences as well. In what could be described as one of the toughest cities in the world for a restaurant and bar to survive over the years, Sardi's has surely made its mark.

It was at Sardi's several years ago, after attending the opening of *Side by Side by Sondheim*, that I was first shown that adding whisky to a fruit sour actually enhanced the flavour of the cocktail. There are many popular cocktails which are served at Sardi's but one which is unusual and special at this bar is named Iced Tea, even though tea does not even become part of the ingredients.

Iced Tea *(left)*

1 measure gin
1 measure vodka
1 measure rum
1 measure Cointreau
1 measure tequila
1 measure lemon juice

Shake the ingredients well with ice and pour into a large highball glass. Top up with Coca-Cola. The presentation of this can be enhanced with either a wedge of lime or lemon on the glass. It should be sipped through straws.

Another favourite cocktail at Sardi's is this delicious almond-flavoured drink which can be served also with whole almonds as an additional touch.

Toasted Almond *(far left)*

1 measure Kahlua
1 measure Amaretto
1 measure cream

Shake with ice. Strain into a cocktail glass or champagne saucer. Serve with a small dish of toasted whole almonds on the side.

has changed but also the customer has changed as well. Whereas once the cocktail bar was the haven of the privileged few, now, with the surge of interest in cocktails and the opening of new bars in towns and the suburbs of major cities, cocktails are available to everyone. Even many supermarkets now stock pre-mixed cocktails which, although timesavers, cannot compare with the real thing.

Even more recent than this latest revival of cocktails is the current fashion for champagne. Always a universally popular drink, champagne is now suddenly enjoying a much greater degree of popularity than it has for some years. This delightful wine from the north-eastern part of France is of course a divine drink on its own but it is now used increasingly as a finishing touch to many cocktails, creating a style that has much panache.

The world of cocktails offers many opportunities for experimenting with less well known liquors from the various corners of the world. One which is at present making a name for itself is saké, from Japan. Traditionally, this strong rice wine is served warmed in special porcelain cups, but recent experiments have revealed that this can make an interesting ingredient in a cocktail. Care should be taken when experimenting with this wine as, for those not familiar with it, saké has a rather oily or sweaty consistency. Once the palate has become accustomed to this it proves to be a delightful and refreshing drink.

The cocktails contained in the following pages include some which may contain liqueurs or spirits that may not be easily available in your local drinks store, but with a little persistence these should be obtainable and will prove interesting conversation pieces and new taste experiences! Well worth remembering too, is that when travelling abroad you can discover, with the assistance of a helpful local bartender, spirits, liqueurs, juices and recipes which may only be available in that part of the world and if brought back home would add unusual recipes to your cocktail repertoire in your own part of the world. So, whether it is Arak from Indonesia or Kava from the South Sea Islands, don't be afraid to try a little experimentation to create a cocktail that could be the envy of many of the barmen in some of the world's leading bars and hotels.

The very name of Zanzibar conjures up visions of exotic locations in far flung corners of the world and, maybe, this was the original concept for this famous bar/club in the heart of London's Covent Garden. Zanzibar was the forerunner of the trend of new wave cocktail bars which were to sweep through London's West End several years ago, and it is one of the few that has endured the vagaries of the capricious cocktail clientèle. The most obvious reason for this is the high standard of cocktails and general service that every client is offered. What is less apparent is the great amount of thought and planning that has gone into making this bar one of the most chic and successful in London.

Because Zanzibar is a private club it is only possible to visit as a member or as a guest of a member. Once inside, however, you are admitted to a different world. The colourful décor of mainly yellow and lime green creates a sunny atmosphere. There are quiet tables available for a business talk or romantic tête-à-tête. The bar is cleverly designed in a zig-zag fashion which makes for easy conversation and the staff are selected not only for their skill as barmen but also for their personality. You may find yourself being served by an artist, writer or more often than not, one of the many out of work actors that abound in this area.

The clientèle at lunchtime tend to be from the worlds of journalism and fashion but at night the club attracts a wide variety of personalities from London's West End. Each Christmas the decoration of the club takes on a new and exciting theme which is designed by a well-known British film animator.

Zanzibar has several cocktails which are particular to the club but here we have chosen two popular cocktails for which we give Zanzibar's own special recipes, so that you can serve them to your friends exactly as they would be served to you in Zanzibar itself.

Zanzibar Mai Tai *(left)*

1 measure dark rum
1 measure apricot brandy
1 measure orange Curaçao
1 measure lime juice
2 dashes orgeat syrup

Place all the ingredients into a blender with ice and blend until smooth. Pour into a goblet or highball glass and decorate with a wedge of lime and a maraschino cherry and two thick straws.

New Orleans Punch *(right)*

1 ½ measures Bourbon
¾ measure dark rum
1 measure orange Curaçao
2 measures lemon juice
½ measure framboise

Stir the Bourbon, rum and lemon over crushed ice in a large glass. Pour on the Curaçao and add the framboise or raspberry syrup.

The fashionable and popular bar of Arthur's is situated in downtown Sydney in the area known as Potts Point. This delightful bar is decorated in a 1950s contemporary style and although the bar itself is not large it becomes a mecca for not only clientele living in the immediate vicinity but also for patrons who travel some distance to sample some of the delicious creations that are prepared at the bar.

Not only does Arthur's have a good and comprehensive cocktails and drinks list but also a menu which can offer snack foods or a full meal. A feature well worth noticing is that all the fruit juices are freshly squeezed to order and it really is a delight to see freshly squeezed mango and papaya juices as well as the juices more usually served. The ideal climate of this region of Australia makes it extremely easy to obtain some of the more exotic fruits for the fruit cocktails for which this particular bar is well-known.

The recipe below is special to Arthur's and once again shows that, with a little imagination, any bartender can invent a drink especially for his or her own bar.

Arthur's Day Dream
2 measures tequila
1 measure lemon juice
½ measure fraise syrup or liqueur
(depending on how strong you like
your cocktail to be)
5 large strawberries
Soda to top up
Blend all the ingredients together with three to four ice cubes and then top up with soda. Decorate with a slice of lime and a strawberry and sip through two large straws.

GLOSSARY

The following list describes the many different kinds of liquor used for making cocktails. Specific terms related to methods and serving are defined in detail on pages 32 to 37.

Advocaat A Dutch liqueur made of sweetened egg yolks and brandy.
Almond Syrup *See* orgeat
Amaretto A legendary Italian liqueur made from almonds, citrus fruit and vanilla.
Angostura Bitters A rum base flavoured with herbs, from Trinidad.
Anisette A sweetened form of Pastis.
Apricot Brandy Pure grape brandy flavoured with dried apricots.
Applejack An American form of the French Calvados, but with less subtlety.
Armagnac *See* Brandy
Bacardi A white rum originally from Puerto Rica, now produced in Spain, Mexico and Brazil.
Bananes (Crème de) A banana-flavoured liqueur.
Benedictine A liqueur from herbs made to a secret recipe by the monks of Fécamp in Normandy.
Blackberry Brandy A mixture of pure blackberry juice with brandy.
Bourbon A maize whisk(e)y originally made in Bourbon County, Kentucky, USA. This whiskey is aged in charred oak barrels.
Brandy A distillation of grape juice, aged for three years. Cognac is a brandy from the Cognac region of France. Armagnac, now increasing in popularity, is a brandy from the Armagnac region of France.
Cacao (Crème de) This is a chocolate and vanilla-flavoured liqueur. Available brown — an extract of pure cacao, or white — a distillation of pure cacao.
Calvados A pure apple brandy from France. The best is produced in Normandy and drunk when over ten years old.
Campari A red Italian bitters served as an aperitif.
Capricornia An Australian liqueur made of a blend of exotic fruits mixed with a local spirit with a resemblance to tequila.

Cassis A blackcurrant alcholic or non-alcoholic cordial, also known as crème de cassis.

Champagne French sparkling wine from the Champagne region of France, mostly made from the Chardonnay, Pinot Noir or Pinot Meunier grapes.

Chartreuse Another secret herb recipe, this time from the monks of the Carthusian order in the region of Grenoble, France. The green Chartreuse is stronger in alcoholic content than the yellow, but not as sweet.

Cherry Brandy A liqueur made from sweet dark cherries, French brandy, Kirsch, herbs and syrup. De Kuyper Cherry Brandy has been made in Holland since 1695.

Chocla Menthe A liqueur made from cacao and peppermint.

Cider An alcoholic or non-alcoholic beverage made from apples.

Cocoriba A coconut based, rum liqueur.

Cognac See Brandy

Cointreau The most famous of all the orange Curaçaos (See Triple Sec) It is made from oranges and served as a liqueur.

Curaçao A liqueur made from the peel of oranges. The name hails from the island in the West Indies. Curaçao can be orange, green blue or white. It is similar to Triple Sec, which is the second distillation.

Drambuie One of the oldest liqueurs in the world made from whisky, honey, herbs and heather.

Dubonnet A sweetened, fortified wine sharpened by the addition of quinine. Served as an aperitif.

Fernet Branca A strong Italian aperitif recommended as a hangover cure!

Fraise Available either as a non-alcoholic cordial or as a liqueur made from strawberries.

Framboise A non-alcoholic cordial or liqueur made from raspberries.

Forbidden Fruit An American liqueur made from apple, honey, orange and a type of grapefruit.

Galliano A yellow Italian liqueur for which the recipe is secret. It first became popular with the advent of the Harvey Wallbanger but is now increasingly used in other cocktails, is drunk straight or used in cooking.

Genever Dutch gin which is much heavier than English gin. Mixes well with Coca-Cola.

Gin A distillation of grain with a flavour of juniper berries and coriander.

Golden Heart Curaçao, orange peels and gold flakes.

Gomme Syrup A mixture of sugar and water. It can be produced by boiling 1 lb (450 g) sugar in 1 pint (56 cl) water.

Grand Marnier A curaçao type of liqueur based on fine cognac with a distinctive orange flavour.

Grenadine A red non-alcoholic syrup produced from pomegranates.

Irish Whiskey A whisk(e)y made from a mash of malted and un-malted barley with wheat, rye and oats.

Kahlua A strongly flavoured Mexican coffee liqueur.

Kirsch Colourless liqueur flavoured with fermented ripe cherries.

Kummel A liqueur flavoured with caraway seeds.

Lillet A wine aperitif from the Bordeaux region of France flavoured with herbs and a little quinine. It is either red or white.

Madeira A fortified dessert wine produced on the island of Madeira.

Mandarinette A Curaçao type of liqueur, orange in colour and made from mandarins.

Maraschino A liqueur distilled from maraschino cherries.

Marsala A strongly flavoured fortified dessert wine produced in Sicily used mostly in cooking.

Martini See Classic cocktails page 40.

Menthe (Crème de) A mint-flavoured liqueur which is white (colourless) or green.

Metaxa A strong flavoured Greek brandy.

Midori A Japanese melon-flavoured liqueur, green in colour.

Nassau Orange An orange liqueur made from distilled extracts of Curaçao with lemon and orange peels.

Noilly Prat Probably the oldest of all the dry French vermouths.

O Cha A Janapese green tea liqueur comprising of a delicate blend of tea and brandy.

Orgeat A non-alcoholic almond-flavoured syrup.

Parfait Amour A liqueur made from citrus fruits with almond flavouring, violet in colour.

Peach Brandy This is made from fresh peaches and pure grape brandy.

Pastis An aniseed-flavoured liqueur which originated at the same time as Absinthe, and now a term which includes Pernod and Ouzo.

Persico (also known as crème de noyaux) A colourless liqueur made with bitter almonds.

Port A heavy Portuguese wine for which the fermentation has been prematurely arrested and grape spirit added.

Rum A distillation of molasses and ranging from white (clear), light to dark and in proof up to 151°.

Rye Canadian whiskey made with at least 51 per cent rye, and matured in oak casks.

Sabra An Israeli orange and chocolate liqueur.

Saké A Japanese rice wine, traditionally served warm in porcelain cups.

Sambuca An aniseed-flavoured Italian liqueur. It is usually served with two coffee beans floated on top and then ignited, which serves to roast the beans and burn off the alcohol.

Sherry A fortified wine with brandy added. Available as fine (dry), amontillado (medium), and oloroso (sweet).

Sloe Gin An English cordial made from sloe berries. Easily made at home by filling a bottle one third full of sloes, plus 3 oz (85 g) caster sugar and topped up with gin. Shake well and leave for at least three months, shaking regularly. Before serving, decant through a fine muslin cloth.

Southern Comfort An American peach-flavoured whiskey.

Strega An Italian liqueur made from citrus fruits and herbs.

Tequila A spirit of Mexican origin which has rapidly increased in popularity in recent years. It has a pronounced flavour and is made from the juice of a cactus plant.

Tia Maria A molasses-based, coffee-flavoured liqueur from Jamaica.

Triple Sec The second distillation of Curaçao. A colourless liqueur produced from orange peels, similar to Cointreau and becoming increasingly popular.

Vermouth Italian and French aperitif wines flavoured with herbs. Available in ranges from white (dry or sweet), rosé (sweet) and red (sweet).

Vodka A distillation of grain. It is usually colourless but can be obtained in varying colours and flavours, from fruit-flavoured dessert vodka to cayenne-pepper flavoured vodka. A vodka known as Bison is produced in Poland.

Whisk(e)y A distillation of malt, sugar, yeast and grain. Originally produced in Scotland, now made in varying qualities in countries as far afield as Japan.

11

BEFORE YOU BEGIN

The following chapters give advice on everything you need to know to be able to make successful and mouth-watering cocktails. An explanation of all the different kinds of liquors provides a guide to an otherwise bewildering choice. Stocking up – with liquor, equipment, glasses and garnishes, is a vital part of the preparation for cocktail making, even for the beginner's most modest cocktail bar. The different methods – muddling, mixing, shaking – are explained as is how to serve cocktails 'straight up', simply with a 'twist' or with gorgeous garnishes. Whether making cocktails for two or planning a cocktail party, you will want to know all this before you begin.

STOCKING UP

How to stock up a cocktail bar, for the beginner starting out with half a dozen bottles and for the more adventurous wanting to explore the delights of Golden Heart, Midori or Japanese saké. An introduction to the range of other basic essentials for those who can't resist all the mouth-watering creations which follow.

Now is the time to think about stocking up your bar with drinks and it is important at this early stage, if you have not established a well-stocked bar to give some thought to how much you are prepared to spend. To create all the wonderful concoctions that you are about to read about, the outlay for the liquor stock alone for your bar is going to be high. The glossary offers you a complete list of drinks for a bar if you want to have a stock of liquor to create the widest range possible of cocktails. However, even if you want to start your bar off in a small way there are certain items that you must have to begin with. You may then gradually add different items to your bar stock, therefore increasing your versatility and the range of cocktails that you will be able to produce.

The basic items of stock to purchase first should be the five main spirits which are gin, Scotch whisky, brandy, vodka and light rum. Essential for any self-respecting cocktail barman is Angostura Bitters which, in case you were unaware, is an invaluable flavouring in the kitchen as well as the bar. The next items should be a bottle of each of the following: dry vermouth, sweet vermouth and Campari. So now you already have the makings for a Martini, Americano, Rob Roy and several other cocktails, at your fingertips.

For your first liqueurs, De Kuyper Cherry Brandy is always a favourite as is Singapore Sling — a Collins (page 42) with cherry brandy added. This liqueur can of course also be drunk straight as a liqueur on its own or is delicious iced. In addition you will need one of the orange liqueurs, either Cointreau or Triple Sec, then Tia Maria or dark crème de cacao, so that you have the beginnings of the spirit stock of your bar.

Once you have started getting quite a reasonable stock together and have begun making some of the more exotic cocktails then you will want to start thinking about purchasing some of the syrups available. You can of course make your own sugar syrup, (*see* page 11) but if you prefer to purchase this then gomme should be one of your first syrup purchases. Grenadine, the pomegranate red syrup, is essential for colouring. The other syrups can then be added gradually to your collection as you progress.

The fruit juices that you use in your cocktails should be fresh ideally, but this is not always possible. It is easy to make fresh orange juice and fresh lemon juice and in no circumstances should orange or lemon squash be substituted, as the addition of this will ruin a cocktail. Lime juice may be difficult to purchase and fresh limes are not always available, but you can deep-freeze fresh limes when they are in season therefore enabling you to keep a stock all the year round. Extracting juice from some of the more exotic fruits can be laborious and expensive and with the superb quality of some of the brands available on the market it is far more sensible to purchase your juices or nectars ready-pressed. These can be purchased in cocktail speciality shops and most of the leading supermarkets and health food stores. Remember that these products, once opened, only have a short life, even under refrigeration, and therefore should not be used after the expiry date on the carton or bottle. Should you find that you do have some nectars or juices left over at the end of a party, don't throw them away. Mix them all together and pour them into

Left to right: Americano, Rob Roy, De Kuyper Cherry Brandy

an ice cube tray in your refrigerator freezing compartment, or into your deep freeze, and you'll have some great tasting ice cubes to add to some of your drinks.

In the process of stocking your bar you may like to add an item which is perhaps a little more exotic than usual. Saké, the Japanese wine, is currently enjoying increased popularity in Britain and what more novel way of entertaining your guests than by serving them saké in the traditional manner, with the saké warmed and served in porcelain cups? You may even decide to be more ambitious and buy an oriental cookery book so that you can conjure up the magic of Japan by not only offering its drink of hospitality, but also some Japanese foods.

The equipment you will need for cocktail making is dealt with in detail in the next chapter, but the following list of basic items will give the beginner — or those contemplating stocking up a bar, an idea of the basic essentials. The first and most obvious implement is a good bottle opener. The multi-purpose 'waiter's friend' is ideal for beginner or experienced barman. You'll also need a good insulated ice bucket. Glass ones may look very decorative but the ice inside tends to melt very quickly. Next is your measure. You may either purchase a single 2 fl oz (5 cl) measure or a dual purpose measure which has a 2 fl oz (5 cl) measure at one end and a 4 fl oz (10 cl) measure at the other.

Before you stock up you also need to think about cocktail shakers. With all the different types available it is sometimes difficult to choose, depending upon how much you wish to spend initially. The type of shaker that you purchase will influence whether or not you need to purchase a mixing jug, but you will certainly have to purchase a mixing or muddling spoon. You will also need a chopping board which will be kept exclusively for the use of your bar and a sharp knife for preparing the fruit garnishes. With these basic items you now have the beginnings of your bar and as you progress and gain more experience your stock and equipment should increase with your knowledge. One thing to remember is not to be misled by some of the cocktail aficionados who like to lead people to believe that the whole process of making cocktails is a highly complicated procedure. For any craft, whether in

the kitchen or at the carpenter's bench, it is important to be familiar with your tools and equipment and also the substances you are working with. This coupled with a little common sense, a desire to learn and to share your ideas with others, will soon make you a competent and popular dispenser of cocktails, both alcoholic and non-alcoholic.

A good basic stock of bottles for your bar, left to right: a bottle of Campari, De Kuyper Cherry Brandy, Bacardi, Cognac, vodka, whisky. The cocktail is Singapore Sling.

EQUIPMENT

A detailed description of the equipment needed for making cocktails – from cocktail shakers to measures and muddling spoons, how to select, use and look after them to ensure many years of valuable assistance. Not all of this list is essential to begin with but all the items will have a use at some time for the serious bartender.

In addition to the liquid supplies of the bar, and without this you certainly won't get very far – the most important items will be the equipment that you need to produce your cocktails. Although there are always short cuts as well as alternatives for the non-availability of an item, it is infinitely preferable, and certainly more professional, to obtain the best equipment available.

With the increasing popularity of home-produced cocktails many of the larger department stores now stock the various items necessary and in some cities there are specialist shops which deal purely in cocktail equipment for the amateur barman. In these you will always be able to pick up some very useful hints, not only for the preparation and presentation of your cocktails but also for the use and maintenance of your equipment.

It is essential that your utensils are kept at all times scrupulously clean and for this there is no short cut. When washing out your cocktail shaker, or for that matter anything that has had either milk or cream in it, do be sure that all the residue of these dairy products has been completely removed from the piece of equipment. The most effective method for doing this is to have a kitchen washing-up brush solely for the purpose of washing your bar equipment. The items to be cleaned should be immersed into hot water which, ideally, should contain a non-foaming sterilizer. Scrubbed thoroughly with the brush the item should then be rinsed in clear hot water and allowed to drain. Ideally, the water for rinsing should be sufficiently hot to

assist in the drying of the equipment but, clearly, if you are making cocktails one after the other this is not practical as a warmed shaker or blender jug should never be used to make cocktails. Special care should be taken when cleaning the blender as it is in the area around the blades where pieces of fruit may often become entangled. Without due care also a small residue of a blended cream cocktail may lie in waiting for a totally different cocktail which will be ruined if cream is mixed with it.

After a party always make sure that your bar or cabinet has been wiped clean with a damp cloth and that the bottles you have been using to dispense your potions have been wiped down, especially around the pourers or caps, and that all your mixing, blending and shaking equipment has been properly washed, rinsed and is either dried or drying. If you use a glass cloth or tea towel to dry your equipment, extra care must be taken that these are completely clean. It is always preferable to let the pieces of equipment drain dry, finally returning them to their allocated space the following day.

When setting up your home bar it is important that you arrange not only the stock of liquor but also the equipment in such a way that the operation of making your cocktails is as easy as possible. Each item of stock or equipment must be returned to its allocated space each time it is used.

Blender – Liquidizer

If you wish to make any of the blended fruit cocktails then it is essential that

you purchase a blender that is specially designed to do the job that you require rather than a small domestic liquidizer. There are a number of blenders on the market at present which should prove satisfactory. Certain blenders are available with attachments which may prove extremely useful and these attachments may be purchased as extras. Suggested attachments, as additions to your blender base and blending jug are as follows: an ice crusher with two different settings, a juice extractor and a slicer. When purchasing your blender, ensure that it has several blending speeds. The base of the jug, which is of course detachable, should be specially cared for when cleaning to avoid any pieces of fruit that may have been caught beneath the blades. Special

---

A blender is an essential item for making fruit cocktails. Here is also shown a metal pourer.

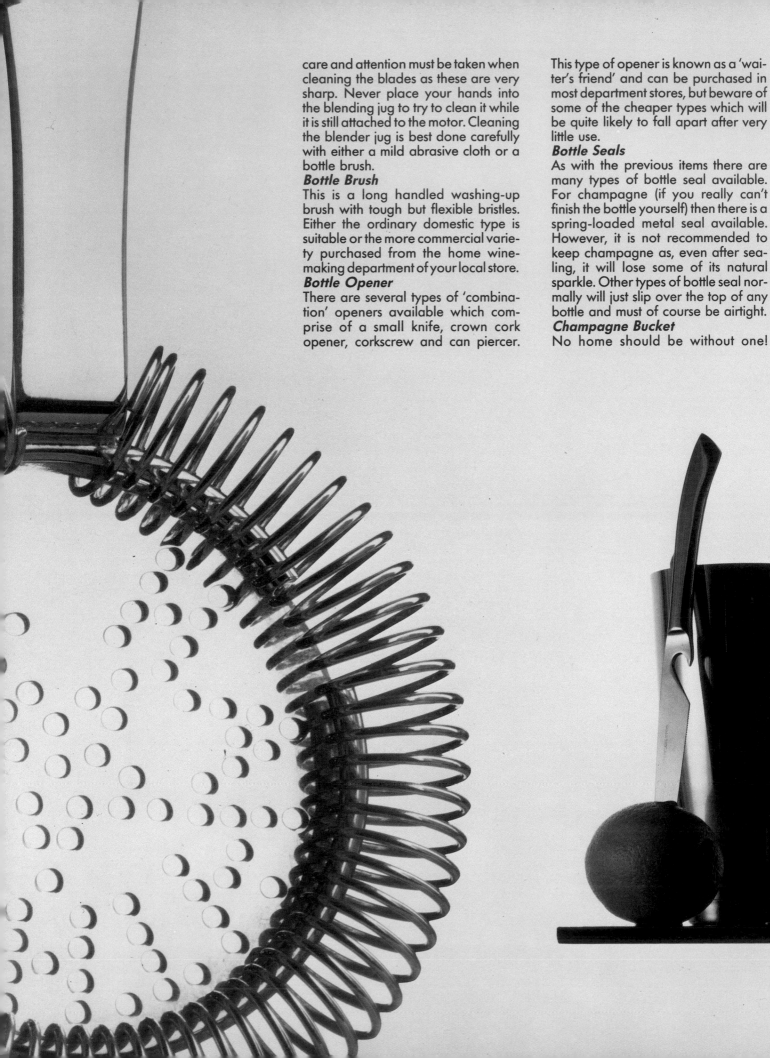

care and attention must be taken when cleaning the blades as these are very sharp. Never place your hands into the blending jug to try to clean it while it is still attached to the motor. Cleaning the blender jug is best done carefully with either a mild abrasive cloth or a bottle brush.

Bottle Brush

This is a long handled washing-up brush with tough but flexible bristles. Either the ordinary domestic type is suitable or the more commercial variety purchased from the home wine-making department of your local store.

Bottle Opener

There are several types of 'combination' openers available which comprise of a small knife, crown cork opener, corkscrew and can piercer. This type of opener is known as a 'waiter's friend' and can be purchased in most department stores, but beware of some of the cheaper types which will be quite likely to fall apart after very little use.

Bottle Seals

As with the previous items there are many types of bottle seal available. For champagne (if you really can't finish the bottle yourself) then there is a spring-loaded metal seal available. However, it is not recommended to keep champagne as, even after sealing, it will lose some of its natural sparkle. Other types of bottle seal normally will just slip over the top of any bottle and must of course be airtight.

Champagne Bucket

No home should be without one!

These conical-shaped buckets are the *piece de resistance* when serving champagne. If required they may be purchased with a metal stand.

Champagne Pliers

Not often needed, hopefully. These are special pliers which will assist in the extraction of the cork from a bottle of champagne. A hint to remember when serving champagne is that the cork should not be pulled out and the champagne allowed to 'pop', but the bottle should be opened with a delicate hiss.

Chopping Board

A plain piece of hard wood which has been well sealed is essential for the preparation of your fruit garnishes. The most convenient size for this is 12in × 6in (30cm × 15cm).

Cloths

Always keep one damp cloth for wiping bottles or spilt drinks. For washing glasses it is advisable to have one cloth for drying and another for polishing, which should preferably be made from linen. It is most important that any cloths that come into contact with your equipment or glassware are clean.

Cocktail Shaker

Cocktail shakers now appear in various shapes and sizes, but the classic shaker remains unchanged. This is a three-part shaker which consists of a base into which the liquor (and ice) is placed, then a cap with a built-in strainer, which fits firmly over the outside of the base, and finally the top which fits over the strainer. Another type available is of American design. This is in two parts consisting of a glass base and metal top which fits just over the top of the glass base. The advantage of this is that you could use the glass base as a mixing jar. However, it does not include a strainer which you would need for cocktails served 'straight up'.

Coffee Machine

Although there are numerous coffee makers available for excellent coffee with which to produce liqueur coffee, there is also now available a small

Some of the most essential items for the different methods of cocktail making, left to right: a Hawthorne strainer, a sharp knife, the metal top of a Boston shaker, a small liqueur glass, a fruit peeler, fruit squeezer, the glass base of a Boston shaker, a metal shaker, the waiter's friend and a blender.

domestic version of the Italian expresso coffee maker.

Corkscrew
See Bottle Openers. However, if you should wish to purchase a plain corkscrew, it is advised that it should be made entirely out of stout metal.

Dash Bottle
This bottle is used for bitters. The only bitters to be sold in a bottle with a plastic nozzle recessed into the neck are Angostura Bitters. The other types of bitters come in ordinary bottles and so if you are not confident enough to pour a dash from a large bottle then this little addition is a cheap but essential part of your equipment.

Dispensers – Pourers
There are several types of dispensers on the market, ranging from metal to plastic. Even the most professional barmen tend to measure their drinks, but there are those who engage in what is called in the trade 'free-pouring'. This means that, by using a dispenser they are extremely familiar with, it is possible to gauge how much liquor to pour. This is not to be recommended unless you are extremely experienced. There are some dispensers that are designed to pour fast and some slowly. The metal topped dispensers with cork bases, which fit snugly into the bottles, are used in most bars these days. However, there is a growing trend towards the plastic dispensers which can be extremely colourful. Unfortunately, however, the plastic

Equipment for muddling and mixing as well as some useful accessories, left to right: an ice bucket, ice container and tongs, a muddling spoon in a mixing jug, an ice scoop, an American 'speed' shaker, to be used in conjuction with the glass in which the drink will be served, a measure, glass jug, a nutmeg grater and shot glass or jigger.

dispenser is likely to last only a few months. It is also very important to keep the dispensers cleaned regularly, removing any residue of the liquor from them. If removed from the bottle for any reason, always make sure that the dispenser is returned to the same bottle.

Fruit Squeezer

This, as the name suggests, is used for squeezing the juice from fruit. The electric attachment to your blender is probably the most efficient method of extracting the juice but also available is a serrated cone onto which each half of the fruit is pressed. Once the fruit has been pressed onto this the juice must then be strained.

Hawthorne Strainer

The true Hawthorne Strainer consists of a flat perforated metal disc which is surrounded by a metal spring with a handle. It is advised to purchase this in stainless steel. It is used for straining the liquid cocktail into the glass without the ice.

Ice Bowl/Bucket

It is essential that this piece of equipment is insulated if you don't have a refrigerator handy.

Ice Crusher

There are several hand and machine models of ice crusher on the market but if not available to you another solution is to wrap up some ice cubes in a clean towel and roll over them with a wooden pastry roller or, better still, beat them with a wooden mallet.

Ice Tongs/Ice Scoop

Two useful pieces of equipment.

Ice Tray

A recent innovation now available is an ice tray made of a form of plastic that does not need to have water run over it to release the ice. All you have to do is twist the tray to release the ice.

Jugs

Cream for mixing should always be kept in a jug which is cleaned out thoroughly every day if in daily use.

Ladle

If serving hot or cold punches you must have a ladle with which to serve your drinks.

Liquidizer See Blender.

Mallet

Unless you have a manual or machine ice crusher you will probably need a mallet. See Ice Crusher.

Measures

When preparing a cocktail it is important to get the quantity of the ingredients right. The standard measure, known as a jigger, is 1½fl oz (4cl). Other measures are also available in different sizes but any small metal or glass receptacle could be used for a measure if you do not have a cocktail measure. The importance of the measure is that it is consistently used for all ingredients specifying it in the recipe.

Mixing Glass/Jar/Jug

A mixing glass is simply a plain glass jar with a capacity for approximately 1½ pints (or almost 1 litre). It should have a lip for pouring. The cocktail is mixed by means of the muddling spoon in this glass or jug and then either strained or poured into a glass for serving.

Muddling/Mixing Spoon

This is a useful item consisting of a long handle with a spoon at one end and a 'muddler' at the other end. The 'muddler' is used to crush mint, sugar and fruit segments.

Pitcher

This is a jug resembling the mixing glass, to be used to dispense water, for example, Scotch and water.

Pourer

see Dispensers.

Punch Bowl

Ideally, punch should be served from a punch bowl. A good punch set is expensive but will include a ladle and special punch glasses. For hot punches, if possible, use a silver bowl and ladle and for cold punches a crystal or glass bowl with matching ladle.

Saké Set

These are obtainable from oriental food shops and from some department stores. To serve saké in the traditional way it must be warmed and served in special porcelain cups.

Shot Glass

This is a 1½ fl oz (4 cl) measure also known as a jigger.

Shredder/Grater

A smaller version of the domestic variety of cheese grater will be needed for grating ingredients such as nutmeg, chocolate or lemon peel.

Sodastream

If you don't want to buy in your own 'sodas' then make your own. A sodastream can be purchased from department stores.

Spoons

Apart from the mixing spoon you will need at least two teaspoons to place flavourings such as sugar, nutmeg or cinnamon into or onto your cocktails.

Swizzle Stick

This is a stirring aid made of fine wires to aerate a drink. It is often used for champagne to give it extra sparkle, although overuse will flatten any carbonated drink.

GLASSES

Glasses suitable for cocktails can vary in shape, size and character so much that they can be chosen to suit mood as much as for the type of drink to be served in them. Use this list as a practical guide – some glasses are simply more suitable than others for certain drinks.

It would seem that almost every day now there are more and more varieties of glasses on sale to the general public, whereas even during the last few years it was quite difficult to obtain certain types of glass. Nowadays the specialist cocktail shops will always stock the glasses for the purist but also some of the more exotic and unusual designs now available.

It is not intended here to give details of the countless variety of glasses but rather to give a guide to the glasses that you should have available to serve any of the drinks that are mentioned in the following pages.

Glasses must be cared for with the same attention you must give the equipment. Never leave glasses lying around at the end of a party. You may not feel like washing them up at the time but it will be a blessed relief the following morning if you have done. If you are giving a party, if possible why not hire someone to take the drudgery of it all out of your hands. There are many agencies who will provide, at a very reasonable cost, a waiter or waitress, butler or maid to attend to your guests. You may of course wish to prepare the cocktails for your guests yourself and the canapés and titbits, but it's a wonderful feeling to know that at least the clearing up has been left to someone else. Glasses, as your equipment, should always be washed in a solution of hot water and a good detergent which also has a sterilizing property and then rinsed in hot water. Ideally the glasses should be left to drain and then if necessary polished with a fine linen cloth. However most of us don't have unlimited stocks of glasses so that if you do have to dry the glasses ensure that you always use a good quality and clean glass cloth.

Listed below are 13 different types of glass of which there are many variations but the ones named are those that you will be most likely to need.

Brandy Balloon
The shape of this glass was designed so that the true connoisseur of brandy could savour the full bouquet of the brandy. The drinker should hold the glass in the palm of the hand so that the brandy may be brought up to body heat before drinking. For a touch of novelty you may care to serve a cocktail in a brandy balloon and indeed some of the more exotic cocktails can look quite spectacular in one of these glasses.

Champagne Flute
The correct glass to serve champagne in so that it holds the effervescence as long as possible.

Champagne Saucer
This came into use during the last part of the nineteenth century – the wide saucer-shape intended to prevent the bubbles going up the noses of the ladies! Even today it is the most widely used of the two glasses for champagne, but not correctly so. It is better used for serving cream cocktails.

Cocktail Glass
This glass was designed with the true cocktail drinker in mind, having a long slim stem that can be held easily so that the warmth from the hand of the imbiber does not warm the cocktail and therefore detract from the taste.

Left a champagne flute, right a Martini glass.

The V-shaped bowl allows the drinker to savour the aroma of the cocktail. These glasses can vary in size from 2fl oz (5cl) to 10fl oz (28cl) but the most acceptable size is the 4½fl oz (13cl) glass. Although still following the classic design there are now also some very attractive glasses made from handcut crystal available in specialist cocktail shops. Using the standard 1½fl oz (4cl) measure already suggested for your cocktails you will find that three of these measures will just fill a 4½fl oz (13cl) cocktail glass, and when experimenting with cocktails this can be a good guideline to work to.

Highball or Collins

This is a straight clear glass, usually 8fl oz (23cl) or 10fl oz (28cl), and can be used for serving either straight sodas, spirit and mix, beers or even long cocktails.

Hoffman

The most commonly used size for these is 10fl oz (28cl) but there are larger sizes. The original use for this glass in the United States was as a beer goblet, but the design lends itself perfectly to the presentation of the blended and fruit-based cocktails as well as beer.

Liqueur

As the name suggests this is a glass to drink a liqueur from. The measure served for a liqueur is 1½fl oz (4cl) so an ideal liqueur glass should be about 2fl oz (5cl).

Pilsner

This glass has been designed specifically for lager or pilsner-type beers, but it can be used as an alternative to serve the more exotic of the cocktails.

Rocks

Also known as the 'old fashioned' glass or simply as a whisky tumbler. This glass usually has a capacity of 5fl oz (14cl) and, as the name suggests, is used for serving cocktails 'on the rocks'.

It is also used for some spirits, for example Scotch Whisky with a little water and pink gin.

Sherry

Sherry glasses can be of varying shapes and sizes, although the true sherry glass is known as a capita. However, the more frequently used glass for sherry is a double size liqueur glass holding about 4fl oz (13cl).

Tankard (Glass)

A tankard is a glass with a handle. Glass tankards range in size from the ¼ pint (12cl) punch tankard to the ½ pint (25cl) beer tankard and finally to the pint (56cl) tankard. They are available in different types of design from the dimpled version to the clear glass, which is recommended for the serving of Black Velvet.

Wine Glasses

So much has already been written and said by different experts about wine glasses but, ultimately, it is still very much a matter of personal choice. There are, however, a few guidelines to follow which may be of assistance.

Red wine should be served in an 8fl oz (23cl) goblet which will enable the drinker not only to be able to savour the full bouquet of the wine, but also to allow the wine to 'breathe'. White wines are better served in a slightly smaller glass, usually about 6fl oz (17cl) and the white wine glass usually has a slightly longer stem than the red wine glass.

The white wines of Germany are served in glasses with the stems coloured either brown or green, depending on the region from which the wine came. The stems are usually about 5in

The impressive row of glasses includes several variations as well as the basic glasses you will need for the different types of cocktail as specified in the recipes, left to right: a cocktail glass, suitable for cream and fruit cocktails; a rocks or small highball glass; a champagne flute; a champagne saucer; a brandy glass; a small champagne saucer; a large cocktail or fruit cocktail glass; a spirit cocktail glass. Next, a highball glass; an aperitif or port glass; a large wine goblet; a highball glass with a glass stirring rod; a spirit cocktail glass; a shot glass; a pilsner glass; a sherry, aperitif or cream cocktail glass and, finally, a rocks glass.

(12½cm) long.

The choice of your glasses is a very personal one but when purchasing glasses for your home try to avoid buying a glass because it has an unusual shape or colour. Think about what you are going to serve in it and whether it will improve the look of the finished cocktail. You may invent a cocktail of your own in which case you will want to present it in a glass that will enhance its qualities. Whichever glasses you prefer, always be prepared to search around for something a little special, either in cocktail shops or anywhere that you might find antique or unusual glasses to add to your stock.

GARNISHES

The cocktail garnish no longer stops at the cocktail cherry or the discreet olive – though there are certain classic cocktails for which nothing else would be appropriate. Lemon grass, parasols, and sparklers may seem unlikely companions to any drink, but cocktails are all about fantasy, so, be outrageous – with discretion!

With the ever-increasing popularity of home cocktails many manufacturers of bar novelties are now producing garnishes suitable for cocktails made at home. There are non-toxic fireworks, 'crystals' that will glow at the base of a cocktail and even silver personalized cocktail stirrers, for the connoisseur.

The garnish or decoration of a cocktail is very much a personal thing and provides a wonderful opportunity for individual flair and invention. Although there is no hard and fast rule with regard to garnish there are certain cocktails, such as the Martini and its derivations, which call for a certain type of garnishing, such as a twist of lemon, an olive or, as in the case of the Gibson, a pearl onion.

Do not worry or discount a cocktail simply because you do not have at hand the garnish suggested. There are now so many different types of decoration, other than the edible variety, available from cocktail shops that even the most simple drink can be transformed into an outrageous creation quite easily. When creating an exotic cocktail let your imagination run wild but try not to allow your cocktail to become an overblown fruit salad or imitation of an outrageous Easter bonnet! Never overdress a cocktail.

Slices of orange and lemon and a cherry on a stick are the most frequently used garnishes. With the increasing availability of more exotic fruits, such as fig bananas, mangoes, paw paw and many others, many more variations are possible.

When preparing garnishes for your own cocktails, unless you are sure that all the garnishes will be used, try to select garnishes that you will be able to store and use at another time if necessary. There are certain fruits, such as oranges, lemons and limes, that you will be able to deep freeze in the form of slices or segments. Deep freezing is an ideal way of keeping fruit, so you may be able to purchase some of the more unusual fruits when they are in season and freeze them until needed at a later date. Some garnishes, such as parsley or fresh mint, could be grown easily in your kitchen. If you have a friendly greengrocer then he may be persuaded to obtain for you some of the more exotic fruits that he would not usually get in stock. Delicatessens and oriental food stores are very good sources of, not only unusual fruit to garnish your cocktails with, but also unusual fruit juices or nectars.

A form of garnishing is the rimming of a glass with a salt or sugar base. The only cocktails for which you will need to have a salt base are the Margarita and Salty Dog. Rimming with salt is an extremely simple process. All you need to do is to take a wedge of lime and rub it around the rim of the glass. Then dip the rim lightly into the salt which has been placed on a saucer or plate. For some of the exotic sweet cocktails, rimming may also be used to garnish the glass by dipping the rim of the glass first into egg white and then into caster sugar. If you want the glass to be a little more colourful dip the rim of the glass into a mixture of one of the coloured syrups and then the caster sugar.

Rimming a glass is sometimes confused with frosting which has a quite different effect. Frosting is simply the process of chilling the glass before serving a cocktail.

Ideally, any glass that you would use to serve a cold cocktail in, should be chilled in a refrigerator for two to three hours before using. At home this is often a little difficult but certainly the next time you are planning to serve a little champagne for two be sure to chill the glasses well beforehand.

There are many more garnishes than are mentioned here, but the following suggestions for decoration may be used as a guideline.

Almonds
Use either whole or flaked. These can be served whole on the base of the stem as something to nibble, or as flakes gently floating on the top of a cream cocktail.

Apples
Green and crisp or red and rosy, apples are super to float in punches and long cool summer drinks. Remember that to prevent the apple from changing colour after it has been cut you must coat it in lemon juice.

Bananas
These are more easily used for making a blended banana daquiri, but if you should wish to use a slice of a banana as a garnish it must be coated with lemon juice, to prevent discolouration.

Celery Salt
Some say that this is essential for the making of a Bloody Mary. It does certainly lend a nice touch to the finish of a savoury tomato cocktail.

Cherries
Fresh cherries are wonderful to use for decoration but don't forget the stone.

Cocktail Cherries

The most popular cocktail cherries are marinated in Maraschino but there are others available which may be red, green, yellow or blue!

Coconut

Dessicated coconut is good for sprinkling onto the top of some of your more exotic creations. The whole coconut is a novel way in which to serve a rum punch if hollowed out correctly.

Coffee Beans

Probably the only time you will use these is to serve a Sambuca, where the beans burn on top of the liqueur.

Confectioner's Fruit or Flowers

These can be either real flowers such as violets, or moulds of flowers made in fine sugar. A surprise way to serve champagne is drop a confectioner's flower into the glass as you serve it and watch it dissolve in the bubbles.

Crystallized Fruit

This is extremely decorative and always available from your local grocer or patisserie. Such fruits are best attached by a cocktail stick as they tend to sweeten your cocktail considerably if immersed in liquor.

Floaters

This is the American term for cocktail mats. The trend for well-designed mats is now becoming big business and these may even be personalized with your name on one side and your favourite cocktail on the other.

Flowers

Flowers and flower petals make delightful decorations for any drink, but take care that the blossom that you are putting into your loved one's cocktail is not harmful!

Fruit

Fresh fruit is always the best kind of fruit to use to garnish your potions or, when not available, fresh fruit that you have frozen when in season. Fruit which has been preserved in syrup lacks the body to look good for garnishing a cocktail, or is so sweet, due to the immersion in sugar syrup, that it is too sweet to eat.

Fig Bananas

These resemble a small banana and taste delicious. Red in colour they make very interesting decorations.

Ginger

Either root ginger or crystallized stem ginger can make interesting additions to your cocktail. A small piece of crystallised stem ginger on a cocktail stick as part of the Brandy Alexander is an interesting experience!

The classical, simple cocktail garnish – a maraschino cherry on a stick.

Kumquats

These are interesting Japanese small oranges which are also used in Greece to make a delicious liqueur of the same name.

Lemons

One of the most used fruits for garnishing. For quick use, slice some lemon and place it into a plastic bag in your deep freeze compartment. Lemon twists for Martinis are simple to make. Using a sharp paring knife shave off a thin strip of the coloured part of the peel. Each strip should be approximately 1in (2.5cm) long. True professionals then twist this peel over the surface of the cocktail which then releases a spray of the 'zest' of the lemon onto the cocktail.

Lemon Grass

This is not so easy to obtain from your local greengrocer but easy to grow. Any garden shop should be able to obtain this for you. A definitely different way to garnish a Bloody Mary or New England.

Lemon Juice

As with all fruit juices, this must be freshly made. There is no substitute for freshly made lemon or orange juice in the making of cocktails. Under refrigeration fresh juice will store for up to three days.

Limes

At certain times of the year this fruit can be expensive but it will freeze and the juice of a fresh lime is delicious mixed with plain mineral or soda water.

Maraschino Cherries

The real maraschino cherry is the classic cocktail cherry. It is bottled in a special liquor and is red in colour.

Melon

The melon flesh can be scooped out with a Parisienne cutter which will make melon balls with which to decorate your drink. The shell, if hollowed correctly, can be an unusual way to serve one of your more exotic cocktails or fruit punches.

Mint

If floated in a summer cool punch mint will add a delicate but fresh tang to your drinks. If used as a garnish just hang it over the side of the glass.

Nutmeg

A pungent spice which must be used carefully. Nutmeg can be bought already ground or as a nut. It is ideal added to a hot or cold punch or sprinkled on top of a Brandy Alexander.

Olives

Use either green or black olives but use the green one for preference in a Martini. A true Martini should have the olive stuffed with a little pimento.

Onions

A cocktail or pearl onion is the simple

30 When more than a simple cherry is called for — from left to right: grapes, limes, nutmeg, tea, strawberries, pineapple, kumquats, lemon grass, oranges, dessicated coconut, coconuts, pretzels, stuffed olives, cherries, pearl onions, salt, almonds, lollipops, straws.

garnish which converts a Martini to a Gibson, but also proves to be very popular as a nibble with cocktails.

Oranges

This popular garnish provides juice and decoration. Orange juice will keep three days under refrigeration. Sliced orange will also freeze if you wish to keep a good back up supply.

Parasols

Small multi-coloured paper parasols can add an oriental touch to the decoration of any cocktail. They are available from specialist cocktail shops.

Paw-Paw

This exotic fruit must be used very carefully as any addition of the skin to a cocktail could taint the taste.

Pears

These are not often used as a decoration but for a cocktail with a delicate taste this fruit can make an interesting garnish. If you wish to prepare this fruit in advance then it must be coated in lemon juice to stop discolouration.

Pepper

Ground black pepper should only be used in making the savoury cocktails such as the Bloody Mary or New England.

Pineapple

This is certainly one of the most exotic looking of all the tropical fruits. If used in blending ensure that all the outside skin has been removed as this will not only make the drink very bitter but also wrap itself around the blades of the blender. This fruit does not store well in a deep freeze.

Pretzels

This delicious American cocktail snack can be served with any drink. It is a small bread-like straw baked with sesame seeds.

Salt

Use salt for flavouring savoury cocktails and for rimming Margarita and Salty Dog glasses. It is most important that you label your containers of salt and sugar clearly!

Spices

Nutmeg and cinnamon may be used for adding that extra spice to some of your cocktails, particularly cocktails with cream.

Stirrers

Plastic stirrers are used partly as decoration, but also for advertising in bars all over the world. These can be obtained in silver for the cocktail enthusiast who has everything.

Strawberries

A very colourful garnish to add to a summer punch or of course to a strawberry daquiri. These should be used as soon after purchasing, or picking, as possible. They do not freeze well.

Straws

These now come in a variety of colours and designs and are made in a variety of materials including paper, plastic and even glass, although the glass straws are not recommended for obvious reasons. The best straws to use are the plastic 'bendy' variety.

Sugar

Caster sugar is preferable to granulated sugar for use in the making of cocktails, if gomme syrup is not available. It also leaves a better finish when rimming glasses.

Syrup

Various flavoured and coloured syrups are now available. The most popular are the red pomegranate syrup, grenadine, which is almost tasteless; orgeat which is a cloudy almond-flavoured syrup and gomme which is a pure sugar syrup. You can make your own gomme by boiling equal parts of sugar and water and then simmering for one minute. Allow to cool and then bottle.

Tea

There are not many recipes that call for the use of tea as an ingredient but when tea is needed it should be freshly made preferably from good green tea. Plain iced tea is delicious served garnished with a sprig of mint.

Vegetables

Peeled and cut into fine strips, vegetables may be served alongside one of the savoury cocktails or served in a separate dish as crudités, with a dip. The best vegetables to use are celery, carrot, endive, chicory, green and red peppers, cauliflower fleurettes, turnip. These may be prepared well in advance and left in plain salted water until required for use.

METHODS & SERVING

Blending, mixing, muddling and shaking are terms with which every cocktail maker will become familiar –

essential methods that, if applied to the wrong cocktail could be disastrous, and yet so simple once learned.

Hints on serving and storing pre-mixed cocktails are given, with guidance for the cocktail party.

I have written a great deal about all the different ingredients and equipment you will need for cocktails. Now to a basic explanation of the methods by which a cocktail can be made.

Apart from the cocktails which contain eggs or fruit, which should be blended, all other cocktails can be either stirred or shaken. To most purists a Martini should only be stirred, but James Bond insists that his be shaken, which, in the view of most dedicated barmen, will only bruise the spirit and detract from the flavour. The different effects of shaking and stirring are that a shaken cocktail will produce a colder and more cloudy drink in appearance than if stirred. The appearance of the stirred cocktail will be clear. It is always best to follow the method stated in the recipe as there is no doubt that alternative methods will have been tried and the method suggested has proved to be the most successful.

Blending

Many recipes require that the ingredients of your cocktail should be placed into a blending jug, or liquidizer, for a few seconds to that they are all blended into one consistency. This same result cannot be achieved by merely shaking the cocktail. Blending gives a cocktail a frothy consistency as a result of the air that has been incorporated into the cocktail. Most recipes containing eggs, and all recipes which contain fresh fruit, will need to be blended. One of the secrets of blending is to blend for the shortest time possible. Over-blending will reduce your cocktail to a watery slush. Another useful hint is not to put whole cubes of ice into the blender but to break the cubes up and use cracked ice. This will not only speed up the process of blending the cocktail but will save a little wear and tear on the blades of the blender. A final word of warning. Never try to blend anything that is effervescent, unless you want to scrape your cocktail off the walls and ceiling!

Mixing

Cocktails which contain clear ingredients usually require mixing. This is done in a plain clear glass beaker or mixing jug with a small lip for pouring. The capacity of this should be approximately 2 pints (approx 1¼l). Place four ice cubes into the mixing beaker and then pour on the ingredients to be mixed. Stir this mixture gently with the long handled muddling or mixing spoon until the contents have become chilled. You will know when your cocktail has become chilled by a film of condensation appearing on the outside of the beaker or jug. If you have to stir a drink that contains anything fizzy then stir only very gently. This will help to preserve the effervescence of the drink. If you stir an effervescent drink briskly it will quickly lose its sparkle. Above all, a mixed drink should only be stirred for the minimum amount of time, as the object of this exercise is to chill the cocktail and not to dilute it with melted ice.

Muddling

If you wish to make an Old Fashioned or a Mint Julep then you will need to know a little about 'muddling'. At the end of your stirring or mixing spoon is a rounded knob and this is what is known as the 'muddler'. You will use the muddler when making a Mint Julep to crush the leaves of mint together with the sugar, or for the Old Fashioned when you crush the sugar with the Angostura Bitters before you add the liquor. After adding the rest of the ingredients to either of the two cocktails you then use the reverse end of the spoon to stir your cocktail.

Shaking

Drinks containing, sugar, eggs, cream, fruit juices or other ingredients that are difficult to mix should be shaken briskly. You may shake your cocktail with either cracked or cubed ice, but what is most important to remember is that as soon as you have finished shaking the cocktail then it must be served straight away. Once the ice starts to melt and dilutes the cocktail then the drink will be ruined. The indication that your drink has been shaken sufficiently to become chilled is when the outside of the shaker starts to perspire.

As you gain more experience you will undoubtedly discover your most comfortable position for holding your cocktail shaker. For those who are a little unsure, it is most comfortable to hold the shaker in front of you with your right hand holding the top of the shaker with a firm grip and the left hand supporting the bottom of the shaker. The action of shaking is by bringing the cocktail shaker in towards your shoulder and then out again, extending your right arm.

Straining

Cocktails which need to be strained are those served 'straight up' or without ice. Some cocktail shakers have a built-in strainer but if you are straining your cocktail from a mixing glass or a

The beautiful layered cocktail
Pousse Café (see recipe page 35).

shaker that does not, you will need to hold a strainer as close to the shaker or glass as possible and then pour into the cocktail glass. Great care should be taken that the strainer is close to the glass to prevent particles of ice or fruit from passing into the cocktail glass. Always ensure that the wires of the strainer are perfectly clean before use.

Pouring

The only drinks that are simply 'straight poured' from the bottle are those served 'on the rocks' such as Scotch on the Rocks. The liquor should never be poured from the bottle any higher than 3in (75cm) away from the glass. The poured drink should not come any closer than ¼in (5mm) from the rim of the glass.

Floating and Layering

This is the art of floating a spirit on top of a cocktail as for, say, a Harvey Wallbanger, when the Galliano is floated on top of the drink. Alternatively in the case of a Pousse Café, a number of liqueurs are layered carefully in a tall thin glass, poured in the order shown in exactly equal amounts: *Crème de cacao, crème de violette, yellow Chartreuse, Maraschino, Benedictine, green Chartreuse and brandy.*

The ingredients should be poured either over the back of a teaspoon or down a glass stirring rod.

Flaming

One of the most spectacular ways of serving some of the more elegant cocktails is to flame them, though of course only if the recipe suggests this. The secret of doing this is to float a little of the liquor to be set alight on top of the cocktail and pour the remainder into a pre-heated dessertspoon and hold over a flame until it catches alight. Then pour the flaming liquor over the top of the cocktail. It is not a good idea to use thin glass if you are flaming a cocktail. When serving the liqueur Sambuca, then usually two or three

Left, a muddling spoon with burning spirit in it to show flaming. Right, a Gibson Martini, a Martini on the rocks and a muddling spoon.

coffee beans are floated on top of the liqueur and these also flame.

Serving

There is always a cocktail for every occasion, whether to celebrate or to commiserate. Cocktails were originally only served between 6pm and 7pm as an early evening drink before dinner, but nowadays cocktails are drunk at any time of the day or night.

As in any business, the world of cocktails has it's own language and nothing can be more embarrassing than a first attempt at ordering a dry vermouth. The brand name of Martini has become synonymous with vermouth and so for the un-enlightened the bartender's response to an order for a 'dry Martini' would probably be 'how would you like it?' Then we get involved in the jargon of 'straight up', 'on the rocks', 'twist or an olive'! So now for a little explanation. A drink served 'straight up', is one that has been stirred with ice and then strained into a cocktail glass so that the liquor is chilled but has not been diluted with melting ice. 'On the rocks' is just the opposite — when a cocktail is served with ice. You should, however, finish the drink before the ice dilutes it too much!

A 'twist' — of lemon — is used not only as a garnish for a cocktail but also to supply a small amount of the oil or zest of the fruit. To make a 'twist', take an oval slice of peel approximately 1in (2.5cm) in length and make sure that all the pith of the fruit has been removed. Hold this over the glass which contains the cocktail and literally twist it between the first finger and thumb. This action will then release a fine spray of oil onto the surface of the cocktail which will impart a delicate but definite flavour to your cocktail. A request for a Martini with an olive is easily understood but the olive, like the onion garnishing a Gibson, should be speared onto a cocktail stick and placed into the cocktail.

The majority of cocktails are designed to be served cold and so, if possible, not only chill your cocktail glasses before serving but also your shaker and mixing glass.

Storing Cocktails

There are going to be occasions when you need to mix cocktails in advance of the time they are to be drunk. For a cocktail party you may wish to make your cocktails in advance to allow for easy and quick service to your guests.

Left: King prawns – delicious as a food accompaniment to a cocktail. Other food ideas which are simple and elegant to serve with your cocktails are shown here with some champagne cocktails (see recipes pages 83 to 87), left to right: Camp Champ, smoked salmon rolls stuffed with asparagus, Classic Champagne Cocktail, Aquilas, orange salmon roe, a bottle of Taittinger champagne.

One word of caution here is not to pre-mix cocktails that have either cream or eggs among the ingredients. Cream and the eggs are liable to separate from the other ingredients if left standing for any length of time.

An invaluable purchase, which will come in handy at picnics too, is a 1 gallon (4½l) vacuum drinks dispenser. Using one of these will enable you to make your cocktail with ice, providing that this is done no more than two hours in advance of drinking. The other alternative method of storing a pre-mixed cocktail is to make your cocktail without ice, but, if possible, to store it in an airtight container in a refrigerator and then add the ice as you serve the cocktail. Obviously, pre-mixing cocktails does save a lot of time at a party but the taste of the finished cocktail does not have the same fresh taste that cocktails 'made to order' will have. If you do wish to store any left over cocktails it is better to store in a clean, labelled glass container with an airtight cap rather than a plastic container.

The Cocktail Party

If you are intending to give a morning cocktail party from which your guests may be going on somewhere for lunch or shopping, then your cocktails should be light in flavour and not too alcoholic. Champagne has been a perennial favourite as the ideal morning drink, whether it be served by itself or as part of a delicious concoction.

Essential for all your cocktails is ice. If you are entertaining on any scale at all then you will have to order ice from a local delivery service. If you are fortunate enough to possess a large deep freeze then you will be able to store home-made ice in it. Always make sure that you have a good stock of glasses available and that you have at least one person, depending on the size of your party, either to be offering your guests replenishment of their cocktails, clearing away and washing used glasses or serving some form of light refreshment.

At whatever time of the day you are entertaining it is a good idea to serve some form of food. The original idea of the cocktail party was that it was a prelude to a meal and canapés would be served with the cocktails. I still feel that these small delicious savouries are the best form of food to offer with cocktails, and should include crudités with a selection of, perhaps, three or four dips. It is much better to offer a smaller selection of well prepared canapés and snacks than to have a mixture of various types. Two or three cold canapés and one hot is usually sufficient for any cocktail party and will probably be quite enough for you to cope with, unless you are fortunate enough to be able to enlist the help of a friend or two to assist you in your efforts. As an alternative to canapés, perhaps you could experiment with some of your own favourite foods. Rolls of smoked salmon stuffed with either caviar or creamed asparagus; plums or apricots stuffed with creamed avocado pear and stilton; broiled scallops en brochette — the list of possibilities is endless and mouth watering, and many recipe books are available to provide you with other ideas.

RECIPES

In the following chapters you will find recipes for many of the old favourites – the classic cocktails, such as the Martini and Manhattan, and many traditional as well as new spirit-based cocktails, which are grouped separately from the exotic cocktails containing fruit or cream. Those which have wine as a base, are grouped together in a section including hot and cold punches but the most sparkling of all are the champagne cocktails – intoxicating even to look at. The non-alcoholic cocktails are for those who really do want to stay sober but still enjoy the fantasy of these wonderful concoctions.

CLASSIC COCKTAILS

Cocktails have changed so much in recent years – they have become more flamboyant and exotic so that, for some, the following traditional classic cocktails of the 1920s, the Martinis, Sours, Collins and Stingers, have retained a simple elegance that rates them high in popularity. Some modern adaptations are included here also.

Quantities *Throughout the recipes in this book the standard measure specified is 2fl oz (5cl), unless otherwise stated. The ingredients given for each recipe are sufficient to make one cocktail only. Simply multiply the ingredients of the cocktail by the number you need to produce. When ice is stated in a recipe four or five cubes is usually quite sufficient. The majority of cocktails, without the addition of mineral or soda waters, or champagne for topping up, usually consist of 6fl oz (17cl) of liquid, which is a useful guideline.*

A special section has been reserved in this book for those cocktails which are distinctive from all others in that they are the true classics of cocktails. These are cocktails that became famous in the days before the bewildering range of drinks, now referred to as cocktails, was invented. These are simple and elegant cocktails which have stood the test of time and still, by many, are regarded as the favourites.

MARTINI

Perhaps one of the simplest and yet one of the most abused of all the cocktails is the Martini. Each and every barman has his own theory as to how much vermouth should be in a Martini cocktail and, in fact, there has been a complete book devoted solely to the Martini. The Martini cocktail was invented some time before the firm of Martini and Rossi started producing a dry vermouth and in those days the French Noilly Prat was used for a Martini cocktail, and is still preferred by some barmen.

A Martini should never be shaken, but very gently stirred in a clear glass mixing jug or jar, with a long handled muddling spoon so that the ice in the mixing glass does not melt into the liquor yet still manages to chill the drink. Traditionally, the Martini cocktail, which was created in 1910 in New York, was served 'straight up'. This means that the liquor is simply strained into a chilled cocktail glass. The original garnish was an olive, but now it is common practice to be offered either a 'twist', which is a fine sliver of lemon, or an olive.

Nowadays a Martini has changed to such an extent that it may be served 'on the rocks', 'naked' – which is simply chilled or iced gin, or as a Gibson, which is the classic Martini garnished with a single pearl onion.

We now have also the very popular Vodkatina which is a Martini based on vodka instead of gin.

Manhattan

Yet another classic cocktail that seems to have variations on its original content is the Manhattan. This was said to have been invented in the United States during the latter part of the nineteenth century, but since then has undergone various transformations.
1 measure rye whiskey
½ measure dry vermouth
½ measure sweet vermouth
1 dash Angostura Bitters

This cocktail, like the Martini, is stirred and not shaken and may be served either 'straight up' or 'on the rocks'. Garnish with a maraschino cherry.

Old Fashioned

This recipe is almost as popular as the Manhattan and is made as follows:
1 measure Bourbon or rye whisky
3 dashes Angostura Bitters
1 sugar cube

Stir the ingredients together well in a tumbler until the sugar dissolves completely and then add two or three cubes of ice which should be just covered by the liquor.

The British version of the Manhattan is known as a Rob Roy and the only difference is that Scotch whisky is used. Although not named, the Irish version should, needless to say, be made with good Irish whiskey.

A classic champagne glass into which is being poured a Gibson Martini.

SOURS

A sour is a drink consisting of any spirit that is shaken with lemon or lime juice, and sugar. A sour is the base of many elaborate cocktails.

Whisky Sour

2 measures whisky
1 measure lemon juice
½ tsp sugar or gomme syrup

Shake the ingredients well with ice and serve 'on the rocks'. Decorate with a slice of orange and a maraschino cherry.

Some prefer to add half an egg white to the mixture before shaking which makes the drink light and frothy.

Fruit Sours

Fruit sours are becoming increasingly popular and the most effective recipe is one from Sardi's, the fashionable restaurant in New York.
1 measure Scotch or Bourbon
1 measure fruit liqueur (of choice)
1 measure lemon juice

Shake the ingredients well with ice and serve 'on the rocks'.

You will notice in this recipe that the sugar has been left out. The reason for this is that the fruit liqueur is exceptionally sweet, making the use of additional sugar unnecessary. Any spirit may be used to make a sour.

Collins

A variation on the theme of the sour is the Collins. This is a drink originally invented by a head waiter of the same name in London, in the nineteenth century.
1 measure gin
Juice of 1 lemon
1 tsp sugar or ½ tsp gomme
1 dash Angostura Bitters
Soda for topping up

Place all the ingredients except the soda into a highball glass and muddle. Add two or three ice cubes and then top up with soda. Decorate with straws and a slice of lemon.

Sidecar

The Sidecar, a variation of a Collins, was originally from the West Indies:
1 measure brandy
1 measure Cointreau or Triple Sec
1 measure lemon juice

Shake the ingredients with ice. Strain into a cocktail glass and decorate with a twist of lemon.

Between the Sheets

This seems to be a natural progression from the Sidecar.
1 measure brandy
1 measure light rum
1 measure Cointreau or Triple Sec
1 measure lemon juice

Shake the ingredients well with ice. Strain into a cocktail glass and serve. Another of the variations of the sour is the Daquiri:

Daquiri

The original Daquiri was a white or light rum sour using lime juice instead of lemon juice, served as a sour. More recently, from the United States have emerged the frozen Daquiris using exotic fruit blended with various rums, fruit liqueurs and ice. The consistency of the drink resembles a runny sorbet, but the taste is usually delicious. As a guideline follow these simple instructions:
1 measure light rum
1 measure dark rum
1 measure orange juice
½ measure fruit liqueur
2oz (56g) fruit of your choice
5 or 6 cubes of ice

Blend together until a smooth consistency is reached and pour into a large goblet. Decorate with pieces of the fruit used to flavour the Daquiri.

Margarita

The Margarita is also a sour. It originates from Mexico and uses tequila, one of the oldest spirits in the world.

1½ measure tequila
1 measure Triple Sec
(preferable to Cointreau)
½ measure lemon juice

Shake all ingredients well with ice and then strain into a cocktail glass which has been rimmed with salt (as described page 28).

It is most important to have just enough salt on the rim of the glass and the most effective way to do this is to rub the rim with a wedge of fresh lime and then dip the glass into a saucer containing fine salt. Some schools of thought insist that the juice should be 50 per cent lime and 50 per cent lemon, but however you make it the Margarita is a drink you will not forget your first taste of in a hurry.

STINGERS

The Stinger is not a drink to be abused and although the classic Stinger should

42

consist of equal parts of brandy and white crème de menthe shaken with ice and strained into a cocktail glass, the brandy may be substituted by any other spirit.

BLOODY MARY

This is a perennial favourite, especially for brunch parties at the weekend. To make a good Bloody Mary it is necessary to prepare this a few hours in advance of serving as it should be served chilled but without ice. The quantities given are per person:

1 measure vodka (preferably Stolichnya or Bison)
1 measure tomato juice
1 dash Worcestershire Sauce
1 dash Angostura Bitters
1 dash lemon juice
Pepper and salt or celery salt

Mix the ingredients well in a glass jug or mixing jar and chill well before serving. If unable to pre-mix this cocktail

then mix the ingredients with ice and strain the liquor off into the glass, which should be a wine goblet decorated with a stick of celery or a bunch of lemon grass.

Bullshot

A variation of the Bloody Mary is the Bullshot which is prepared in exactly the same way but using cold consommé in place of the tomato juice.

Another version is the Bloody Bullshot which contains a mixture of tomato juice and cold consommé. Yet another variation is the New England using clam juice, lemon and vodka, garnished with lemon grass.

Left to right: Apricot Sour, Stinger, Between the Sheets, Daquiri, Bloody Mary.

SPIRIT COCKTAILS

Vodka, gin, rum, whisky and brandy – the five spirits which provide the different characters of the 'true'

cocktails, each of which has a spirit as its base. Here the well-known Harvey Wallbanger and Shanghai Ginn

Fizz are joined by more unusual names – try Okinawa Sunrise made with saké, or Moscow Melon with Midori.

All true cocktails traditionally had a spirit as their base. Nowadays, with the increase in the number and popularity of mixed drinks of all kinds, the term 'cocktail' is used much more loosely to include both wine-based and non-alcoholic mixed drinks. The cocktails included in this section are all based on spirits but are the less exotic members of the cocktail family in that they do not include fruit or cream.

The old favourites such as the Martini and Manhattan were subjects of the last chapter and are all spirit-based cocktails which have endured the test of time and have established themselves as classics.

You will find here, and throughout the next sections, not only many popular and famous cocktails but also many new recipes using interesting new products. In addition to the new recipes I have collected from my own travels, both from talking to professional barmen and experimenting myself with new products and ideas, several of the recipes have been contributed by amateur barmen. This is great encouragement for those of you who like to experiment or have the opportunity to discover new, or seldom used liquors.

The five main spirits used as a base for the different kinds of cocktails throughout are vodka, gin, rum, whisky and brandy. Do remember that there are many variations of each of these spirits provided by both the country of origin and the different brands. You will undoubtedly find that you prefer to use one particular brand of spirit once you have experimented a bit.

The enthusiast who has made a study of cocktails over the years will probably find in the older recipe books, some of which by now are collector's items, recipes with spirits that are not even produced nowadays. You should not despair of these recipes for you may discover that there are modern substitutes. As yet, sadly, nothing has been discovered to take the place of Absinthe. If you see a name in a recipe that is unfamiliar to you, and is not included in the glossary of this book, check with your local bar to see if anyone there knows of it or what the new equivalent is. When visiting some of the older established bars keep an eye on the shelves for bottles with old labels that look as though they have not been used for years. You may discover a relic of a bygone age which you may be able to purchase and add to your collection of spirits or liqueurs which will then be the envy of your friends. It will be interesting to see in 10 or 20 years' time which of the modern cocktails have survived the test of time and are still popular.

The cocktails in this section of the book range from the aperitif type of cocktail, which is best served before a meal, to the cocktails which are a longer drink to be drunk at any time of the day or night. In the same way that recipes here have been invented by amateur barmen, when you feel confident to do so, you too try to create a concoction of your own. If you do so the best guideline that I can give is not to mix two types of spirit together, and remember that you don't have to use full measures of spirits.

When using liqueurs and flavourings don't only contemplate how the

Chichirera – a spirit-based cocktail (see recipe page 49).

drink will taste but also how the different liqueurs or colourings will mix with the spirit base with regard to the final colour of the finished cocktail. I have known some delicious home cocktails which have looked as though they are a product of a junior school laboratory rather than a bar! So, remember that so much of the success of an invention depends upon the presentation as well as the content and taste.

Andante

1 measure gin
1 measure apricot brandy
½ measure Campari
½ measure dry vermouth
1 dash grenadine

Shake all the ingredients well together and strain into a cocktail glass decorated with an apricot segment and a maraschino cherry on a stick.

Après-Midori

1 measure Pernod
½ measure Midori
1 dash lime juice cordial
1 sprig of fresh mint

Fill a rocks glass with crushed ice and pour on the ingredients in the order given and finally garnish with a sprig of fresh mint.

Benedict Arnold

1½ measures rye whiskey
1 measure Benedictine

Shake the ingredients well together with ice and serve either 'on the rocks' or strained into a cocktail glass and 'straight up'.

Betsy Ross

1 measure brandy
1 measure ruby port
½ measure Cointreau
1 dash Angostura Bitters

Shake the ingredients well together

with ice. Strain into a cocktail glass and serve 'straight up' without a garnish.

Black Forest

1 measure De Kuyper Cherry Brandy
½ measure gin
1 dash Maraschino

Shake the ingredients well together and strain into a liqueur glass. Garnish with a black cherry speared onto a cocktail stick.

Bleeding Heart

2 measures Advocaat
1 dash De Kuyper Cherry Brandy

Pour the Advocaat into a liqueur glass and then add the dash of De Kuyper Cherry Brandy on top of the Advocaat.

Brooklyn

1 measure rye whiskey
½ measure sweet vermouth
1 dash dry vermouth
½ measure Campari

Stir the ingredients with ice until chilled and then pour into a rocks glass decorated with a slice of orange and a cherry.

Canada

1½ measures Canadian Club
½ measure Cointreau
2 dashes Angostura Bitters

Mix the ingredients well together with ice in a mixing jug or beaker until sufficiently chilled and then pour into a rocks glass. Decorate with a sprig of mint floating on the cocktail.

Candide

½ measure gin
½ measure dry vermouth
½ measure Orange Curaçao
1 dash Triple Sec
1 dash grenadine

Shake the ingredients well together with ice and strain into a cocktail glass and serve 'straight up'.

Left: A bottle of Golden Heart with gold flakes in it alongside a dash of Angostura Bitters! The cocktails shown are, left to right: Colonial Boy and Claridges (recipes page 49), Bleeding Heart, Brooklyn, Champs Elysée.

47

Left to right: Green Widow (recipe page 50), Dunhill, Chicago, Cincher, Darlajane.

Champs Elysée

1 measure brandy
1 measure yellow Chartreuse
1 dash lemon juice
1 dash gomme syrup
2 dashes Angostura Bitters

Shake the ingredients well together and strain into a cocktail glass with a little crushed ice.

Chicago

1 measure brandy
½ measure Triple Sec
½ measure Persico
1 dash Angostura Bitters

Shake the ingredients together with ice and then pour them into a highball glass with the ice. Top up the cocktail with either soda water or champagne.

Chichirera

1 measure Parfait Amour
1 measure Golden Heart
1 egg white
1 dash lemon juice
1 dash lime juice

Shake the ingredients well together with ice, strain into a cocktail glass and decorate with a small wedge of lime on a cocktail stick.

Cincher

2 measures gin
1 measure De Kuyper Cherry Brandy
Soda to top up

Fill a wine glass with crushed ice. Pour

on the gin followed by the De Kuyper Cherry Brandy and top up with soda.

Claridges

1 measure gin
1 measure dry vermouth
½ measure Cointreau
½ measure apricot brandy

Stir the ingredients until chilled in a glass jug and pour into a rocks glass decorated with a green cherry on a cocktail stick.

Colonial Boy

1 measure Irish whiskey
3 measures hot strong tea
2 dashes Angostura Bitters

Pour the ingredients into a small but thick glass mug, stir well and serve hot.

Darlajane

1 measure Geneva gin
2 oranges, halved and squeezed
1 passion fruit

Scoop out the flesh of the passion fruit and place in a champagne flute. Pour in the orange juice. Add a little cracked ice. Top up with gin poured on to the back of a spoon to achieve three distinct layers. Drink through a straw by pulling the straw slowly up from the bottom of the glass through the layers, so that the ingredients first mix on the tongue. This recipe was invented by the book designer for his girlfriend on New Year's Eve.

Dunhill

1 measure gin
½ measure orange Curaçao
½ measure dry vermouth
½ measure amontillado sherry
1 dash Anisette

Shake the ingredients well together with ice, strain into a cocktail glass and serve 'straight up' decorated with a twist of orange peel.

Embassy Royale

1 measure Bourbon
1 measure Drambuie
½ measure sweet vermouth
½ measure orange juice

Shake the ingredients well together with ice, strain into a cocktail glass and serve 'straight up'.

Etonian

1 measure gin
1 measure Lillet
1 dash orange bitters
2 dashes Persico

Stir ingredients well with ice until chilled and pour into a rocks glass decorated with a twist of lemon.

Fine and Dandy

1 measure gin
1 measure Triple Sec
1 dash orange juice
1 dash Angostura Bitters

Shake the ingredients well together with ice and strain into a cocktail glass and serve straight up.

Foxhound

1 measure brandy
1 measure cranberry juice
¼ measure kummel
1 dash lemon juice

Shake the ingredients well together with ice and strain into a cocktail glass with a little crushed ice and a twist of lemon. This is a variation on an old English cocktail usually served during the hunting season.

Green Widow

½ measure Advocaat
½ measure green crème de menthe
1 measure vodka
Lemonade to top up

Shake the ingredients well together with ice and pour into a highball glass and top up with lemonade.

Harvey Wallbanger

1 measure vodka
Galliano
Orange juice

Fill a highball glass with ice and then add the vodka. Pour in the orange juice to just below the rim of the glass and float the Galliano on top of the cocktail. Decorate with a slice of orange.

Hiroshima

1 measure saké
1 measure tequila
1 measure sweet vermouth

Shake the ingredients together well with ice and pour into a highball glass and then top up with soda. Decorate with a slice of lemon.

Honeymoon

1 measure Benedictine
1 measure Calvados
3 dashes orange Curaçao
1 dash lemon juice

Shake the ingredients well together with ice and serve 'straight up'. Decorate with a ¼ slice of orange and a cocktail cherry on a stick.

Hong Kong Fizz

½ measure gin
½ measure vodka
½ measure tequila
½ measure yellow Chartreuse
½ measure green Chartreuse
½ measure Benedictine
1 dash lemon juice

Shake the ingredients well together with ice and pour into a large goblet and top up with soda. Decorate with slices of lime and lemon speared on a cocktail stick with a cherry.

Jade

1 measure light rum
½ measure green crème de menthe
½ measure orange Curaçao
½ measure lime juice cordial

Shake the ingredients together with ice, strain into a cocktail glass or serve on the rocks decorated with a slice of lime.

A variation on this cocktail is Indian Jade, which is served in a highball glass and topped up with Indian Tonic Water.

Katinka

1 measure apricot brandy
1 ½ measures vodka
½ measure lime juice

Shake the ingredients well together with ice and strain into a cocktail glass half filled with crushed ice. Decorate with a sprig of fresh mint.

Lark

1 measure De Kuyper Nassau Orange
1 measure Scotch whisky
1 dash lemon juice
1 dash grenadine
Fanta orange

Shake all the ingredients, except the Fanta orange, together well with ice and pour all into a highball glass. Top up with Fanta orange. Garnish with a slice of lemon and a slice of orange on a cocktail stick with a cherry.

On the left, a top from a bottle of saké, with cocktails, left to right: Foxhound, Millionairess (recipe page 53), Hiroshima, a bottle of saké, Jade, a bottle of galliano, Harvey Wallbanger.

L'Opéra

½ measure blue Curaçao
1 measure white rum
1 ½ measures grapefruit juice

Stir the ingredients well with ice in a mixing jug and pour with the ice into a highball glass and top with soda.

Marijka

½ measure De Kuyper Cherry Brandy
½ measure vodka
½ measure lemon juice
1 dash orange bitters

Shake the ingredients well with ice and pour into a rocks glass. Garnish with a twist of orange peel.

Melon Driver

2 measures Midori
Orange juice to top up

Left to right: Marijka, Mint Julep, Pink Almond (recipe page 54), L'Opera, Okinawa Sunrise (page 54), Midori Sour.

Into a highball glass with three ice cubes in it pour the Midori and top up with the orange juice. Garnish with a cube of melon and one maraschino cherry speared onto a cocktail stick.

Mexican Melon

1 measure tequila
1 measure Midori
2 measure passion fruit nectar
2 measures orange juice
1 dash grenadine

Shake all the ingredients, except the grenadine, together with ice and then pour them into a highball glass half-filled with crushed ice. Add the grenadine. Decorate with a slice of orange and a maraschino cherry on the side of the glass.

Midori Sour

1 measure Midori
1 measure lemon juice
1 measure Scotch whisky
1 dash Angostura Bitters
White of 1 egg

Shake all the ingredients well with ice and strain into a cocktail glass. Garnish with a cherry on a cocktail stick resting on the glass. To make the cocktail have

a really frothy head then add the white of an egg to the ingredients, prior to shaking.

Midori Tropical

1 measure Midori
2 measures orange juice
2 measures pineapple juice

Place three ice cubes into a wine goblet and pour on the ingredients. A wedge of pineapple and maraschino cherry speared on a stick should then be used to stir the drink.

Millionaire

2 measures rye whiskey
2 dashes grenadine
2 dashes orange Curaçao
2 dashes Pastis
1 egg white
1 dash lemon juice

Shake the ingredients well with ice and strain into a cocktail glass. Serve 'straight up' decorated with a manzanilla olive on a stick.

Millionairess

1 measure light rum
1 measure apricot brandy
1 measure sloe gin
1 dash lime juice

Shake the ingredients together with ice and strain into a cocktail glass. Garnish with a black cherry and a wedge of lime on a cocktail stick.

Mint Julep

2 measures Bourbon whiskey
1 tsp sugar
1 sprig of mint
Soda

Place sugar, mint and a little soda into a highball glass and mash together with a muddling spoon. When well mixed add the Bourbon and two cubes of ice. Top up with soda.

Moscow Melon

1 measure Stolichnya Vodka
½ measure Midori
Lemonade to top up

Pour the ingredients into a highball glass which has been half filled with crushed ice and garnished with a wedge of lime on the edge of the glass.

Moscow Mule

2 measures vodka
1 dash lime juice
Ginger beer to top up

Place four ice cubes into a highball glass with the vodka and lime juice, mix together with a muddling spoon and then top up with the ginger beer.

Negroni

1 measure Campari
1 measure gin
1 measure sweet vermouth

Mix the ingredients well together with ice in a mixing jug and serve either strained into a cocktail glass and garnished with a twist of orange, or poured into a rocks glass and decorated with a slice of orange on the side of the glass.

Off the Rails

1 measure vodka
½ measure dry vermouth
1 dash white crème de menthe
1 dash orange Curaçao

Shake the ingredients with ice and pour into a rocks glass. Garnish with a twist of lemon peel.

Okinawa Sunrise

½ measure saké
½ measure tequila
4 measures orange juice
1 dash Galliano
1 dash grenadine

Shake all ingredients, except the grenadine, with ice and pour into a rocks glass. Add the dash of grenadine to the cocktail. Garnish with a wedge of orange and a cocktail cherry on a stick.

Pall Mall

1 measure gin
1 measure sweet vermouth
1 measure dry vermouth
1 dash white crème de menthe
1 dash orange bitters

Shake the ingredients well with ice and strain into a cocktail glass or pour into a rocks glass.

Parrot

1 measure dry vermouth
1 measure apricot brandy
1 measure yellow Chartreuse
1 dash Anisette

Rinse a chilled cocktail glass with the Anisette. Shake the other ingredients well with ice and serve strained into the cocktail glass garnished with red, yellow and green cocktail cherries speared on a cocktail stick.

Pink Almond

½ measure Persico
½ measure Kirsch
1 measure Scotch whisky
1 dash grenadine

Shake the ingredients well with ice and serve on the rocks garnished with a red cherry speared on a cocktail stick.

R.A.C.

½ measure gin
¼ measure dry vermouth
¼ measure sweet vermouth
1 dash grenadine
1 dash orange bitters

Stir the ingredients with ice in a mixing glass until chilled and strain into a cocktail glass.

Left to right: Parrot, Midori Tropical, Moscow Mule (recipe page 53), Royale, Moscow Melon.

Red Lion

1 measure gin
1 measure Grand Marnier
½ measure orange juice
½ measure lemon juice

Shake the ingredients well with ice and strain into a cocktail glass. Serve 'straight up' and garnished with a twist of lemon and orange speared to a cocktail stick.

Reids Flip

2 measures madeira
1 egg
1 measure double cream
1 dash Angostura Bitters

Place the ingredients into a blender with four or five lumps of ice and blend until smooth. Then pour into a wine glass or goblet and sprinkle the top with a little cinnamon.

Rosé Glow

½ measure gin
½ measure Campari
½ measure Cinzano Rosé
½ measure Triple Sec
1 dash Angostura Bitters

Shake the ingredients with ice and strain into a cocktail glass. Serve 'straight up' and decorate with a maraschino cherry.

Royale

1 measure Canadian Club
1 measure Calvados
½ measure apricot brandy
2 dashes orange flower water
2 dashes Angostura Bitters
½ measure lime juice
Soda

Pour ingredients, except soda, into a mixing jar or jug over ice and stir well with a muddling spoon. When chilled pour all contents into a highball glass and top up with soda. Garnish with a wedge of apple and slice of lemon.

Sakini

2 measures gin
½ measure saké

Shake the ingredients with ice and pour into a rocks glass and decorate with a manzanilla olive.

Sazerack

2 measures Bourbon whiskey
2 drops Peychaud Bitters
4 drops Pernod

Rinse a rocks glass with the Pernod and then add the Bourbon, one lump of sugar and the Peychaud Bitters. Muddle well until the sugar has nearly dissolved and then add three lumps of ice and mix once again. This cocktail is garnished with a twist of lemon and may be served either 'straight up' or 'on the rocks'.

Shamrock

½ measure Irish whiskey
½ measure dry vermouth
  3 dashes green Chartreuse
  3 dashes green crème de menthe

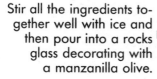

Stir all the ingredients together well with ice and then pour into a rocks glass decorating with a manzanilla olive.

Shanghai Gin Fizz

½ measure gin
½ measure yellow Chartreuse
½ measure Benedictine
½ measure lemon juice

Shake all the ingredients well with ice and pour into a highball glass then top up the cocktail with soda water.

Sixty-Six

1 measure gin
¼ measure sweet vermouth
¼ measure orange juice
1 egg white
2 dashes grenadine

Shake all the ingredients well with ice and then strain into a cocktail glass. Decorate the cocktail with a cherry speared onto a cocktail stick.

Skyline

1 measure lemon gin
1 measure gin
1 measure De Kuyper Nassau Orange
1 measure orange juice
Fanta orange

Into a highball glass place three ice cubes and then add the ingredients in the order which is shown and top up with Fanta. Decorate with a slice of orange and a cocktail cherry.

Sundowner

1 measure white rum
1 measure sweet vermouth
½ measure Calvados
1 dash grenadine
1 dash Angostura Bitters

Shake the ingredients well with ice and then strain into a cocktail glass, serving 'straight up'. Garnish with a small wedge of lemon and a small wedge of orange speared on a cocktail stick.

Tamagozake

6 measures saké
1 egg (lightly beaten)
1 tsp granulated sugar

Place the saké into a saucepan and boil. When the liquor is boiling then ignite it. Remove from the heat and stir in the egg and sugar. Serve in a thick glass mug or thick rocks glass.

Temptation

1 measure Canadian Club
½ measure Triple Sec
½ measure Dubonnet
1 dash Anisette
1 dash lemon juice

Shake the ingredients well with ice and then strain into a cocktail glass, serving 'straight up'. Decorate with a slice of lemon on the side of the glass.

Tantalize

1 measure peach brandy
½ measure lemon juice
½ measure pineapple juice
2 dashes Angostura Bitters
Ginger ale
Grenadine

Shake the ingredients, except the ginger ale and grenadine, with ice and then pour into a highball glass. Top up with ginger ale and finally a drop of grenadine floating on top of the cocktail.

Vanderbilt

1 measure brandy
1 measure De Kuyper Cherry Brandy
1 dash gomme syrup
1 dash lemon juice
1 dash Angostura Bitters

Shake ingredients with ice and then pour into a rocks glass or small wine glass and garnish with a wedge of lemon and a cherry.

Washington

1 measure brandy
½ measure dry vermouth
2 dashes grenadine
1 dash Angostura Bitters
1 dash orange flower water

Shake the ingredients together well with ice and then strain into a cocktail glass with a little crushed ice.

Wedding Bells

1 measure De Kuyper Cherry Brandy
1 measure gin
1 measure Dubonnet
1 dash orange juice
Soda

Mix the ingredients, except the soda, well until chilled with ice and then pour into a highball glass. Top up with soda and decorate with slices of cherry, lemon and orange.

Left to right: Vanderbilt, Skyline, Sakini, Tantalize.

COCKTAILS
WITH FRUIT

The most flamboyant cocktails of all – cocktails made with fresh fruit, not only as a main ingredient but also as a lavish garnish. Reflective of their origins in the West Indies, many of these fruit cocktails have rum as their base. Try Mai Tai or Tequila Sunrise as proven favourites, or Geisha and Haitian Gold for something different.

Any cocktail which contains a fruit flavouring, whether alcoholic or non-alcoholic, could be called a fruit cocktail. This section, however, is dedicated mostly to those exotic creations which include fresh fruit as one, if not the main ingredient, of the cocktail. Fruit-based cocktails originated in the more tropical areas of the world, where there is an abundance of fruits which lend themselves to these flamboyant concoctions. The main creators of the fruit-based, blended cocktails seem to have been in the United States, where the method of blending cocktails first originated. There is also an easy availability of more exotic fruits as the climate is such that nearly everything grows in abundance.

The spirits which lend themselves most to making cocktails with fruit are rum and brandy. Both of these spirits are renowned for their fieriness and yet provide a perfect base for blended fruit. Rum is probably the most obvious of the two spirits to use as it hails from the West Indies, a part of the world which is well known for its tropical fruits and delicious drinks such as the

Pinacolada and Zombie. Because rum is also available in either white, gold or dark brown the range of cocktails it can be used for is infinite. Some consideration needs to be made before using brandy in a fruit cocktail, as unless using a smooth tasting brandy the flavour of the brandy can be quite overpowering.

When selecting the fruit to make a blended cocktail, ensure that the whole fruit is ripe without being over ripe and there there are no blemishes on the skin of the fruit. With most fruits you will have to separate the flesh of the fruit, which will be blended, from the outer skin. It is most important that this is done with extreme care as any addition of skin or pith into the cocktail may produce a sour or bitter taste. Do not peel more fruit than you need and always remember to retain some of the fruit to use as a garnish for your finished cocktail. To stop discolouration of your peeled or sliced fruit, just rub over with half a lemon or just squeeze a little lemon juice over the exposed flesh of the fruit and the acid in this will prevent discolouration. If you cannot find the fresh fruit that is needed to make your chosen cocktail

The exotic fruit cocktail shown here is Apricot Lady (see recipe page 60).

and wish to use canned fruit be warned that the fruit itself will not have the same flavour as fresh fruit, and be sure not to include any of the canned syrup into the cocktail as this will make your drink too sweet.

Before embarking on a fruit cocktail recipe, for which the garnishes are such an important feature, take the time to read through the recipe method to see the type of garnish suggested. Although not essential to the basic list of ingredients, to have the suggested garnishes available — or something similar — will make all the difference to the finished effect.

Apricot Lady

1 measure light rum
1 measure apricot brandy
¼ measure orange Curaçao
½ egg white
2 chopped and peeled apricots
½ measure lime juice

Blend all the ingredients with ice until smooth and then pour into a large goblet which has been decorated with a slice of orange and slices of apricot. The apricot should be coated in lemon juice to prevent discolouration.

Bachanal

1 measure light rum
½ measure brandy
½ measure yellow Chartreuse
1 measure orange juice
½ measure lime juice

Shake all the ingredients well with ice and then pour them into a large goblet which has been garnished with slices of lemon and orange and blue crystallized flowers.

Blue Hawaii

1 measure light rum
½ measure blue Curaçao
2 measure pineapple juice
2 measures Malibu

Blend all the ingredients with ice until smooth. Pour into a halved pineapple or coconut shell with sparklers set into the side. Light the sparklers to serve.

Calypso

1 measure orange Curaçao
1 measure port
1 measure dark crème de cacao
1 measure 151° proof rum

Shake the Curaçao, port and crème de cacao with ice. Fill a grapefruit shell with crushed ice and strain the cocktail into it. Place a lime shell in the centre and fill with rum and then ignite.

Caracas

A cocktail to be shared:
1 measure gin
1 measure green crème de menthe
2 measures pineapple juice
1 measure Triple Sec
1 dash Anisette
1 dash Angostura Bitters

Hollow out an Ogen melon shell using the flesh to make melon balls. Fill the shell with cherries and sliced kiwi fruit. Shake ingredients well with ice, and then pour into the melon shell, or shake without ice and place in a refrigerator before serving.

Cascade

1 measure gin
½ measure Mandarinette
½ measure De Kuyper Cherry Brandy
1 dash kirsch
1 egg white

Blend the ingredients with ice until smooth and then pour into a tall glass decorated with the four black cherries and mandarin orange segments.

Conchita

1 measure tequila
½ measure dry vermouth
½ measure pineapple juice
1 dash grenadine
1 dash orange bitters
2 sliced kiwi fruit

Shake the liquid ingredients well with ice and then pour into a rocks glass and mix with the sliced kiwi fruit.

The sensational Blue Hawaii cocktail is afire with sparklers. Left to right are: Cascade, Geisha (recipe page 62), Caracas, Haitian Gold (page 62).

Corcovado

1 measure blue Curaçao
1 measure tequila
½ measure Drambuie
Soda to top up

Shake the ingredients well with ice and then pour into either a goblet or highball glass filled with crushed ice. Top up with soda. Decorate with the slices of lemon and lime speared on the side of the glass with a cocktail stick.

Dusky Maiden

1 measure Kahlua
1 measure dark rum
3 scoops rum and raisin ice cream

Blend the ingredients together for 30 seconds and then pour into a large goblet. Garnish with slices of fresh peach and 12 maraschino cherries around the edge of the glass. Cinnamon should be grated over the top.

Egril

1 measure dark rum
1 measure white rum
1 measure Irish Mist
3 measures pineapple juice
1 chopped lime

Blend all the ingredients together with ice until smooth and then pour into a highball glass or goblet. Decorate with a slice of lime speared with a cherry on either side of the glass.

Frozen Fruit Daquiri

1 measure light rum
1 measure dark rum
1 measure orange juice
2oz (56g) fresh fruit of your choice
½ measure of fruit liqueur or flavouring

Blend all the ingredients with ice until smooth and then pour into a large goblet. Decorate with slices of the fruit which has been used to flavour the Daquiri, on the side of the glass.

61

Geisha

1 measure O Cha
1 measure saké
½ measure lemon juice
1 measure orange juice
1 measure passion fruit juice
or nectar
4oz (115g) peeled kiwi fruit

Soak the peeled kiwi fruit in the O Cha
and saké overnight and then blend
with the other ingredients and ice the
following day. Serve in a highball
glass decorated with sliced kiwi fruit.

Haitian Gold

1 measure light rum
½ measure De Kuyper Nassau Orange
½ measure tequila

½ measure crème de banane
1 measure guava nectar
1 dash fraise

Decorate a large goblet with red
banana (coated in lemon juice) and
slices of guava. Blend all the ingredients with ice until smooth and then
pour into the goblet.

Hannibal Palace

1 measure whisky
½ measure Drambuie
½ measure orange Curaçao
1 dash Parfait Amour
½ measure guava nectar
½ measure pineapple juice
1 dash lemon juice
1 dash orgeat

Shake the fruit juices and Parfait
Amour together with ice. Strain into a
large wine goblet which has been half
filled with crushed ice. Place the shell
of a mandarin orange in the goblet, fill
with the liquor and ignite.

Left to right: La Mamba, Mai Tai, Hannibal Palace, Julia, Kojak.

Harlequin

1 measure light rum
½ measure Kirsch
½ measure apricot brandy
1 measure orange juice
4 chopped maraschino cherries

Decorate a highball glass, which has been rimmed with grenadine and sugar, with black cherries and crystallized orange. Shake the ingredients together and pour into the decorated glass.

Julia

1 measure white rum
1 measure Amaretto
1 measure double cream
2oz (56g) fresh strawberries

Blend all the ingredients with ice until smooth and then pour into a wine goblet which has been garnished with three strawberries set onto the rim.

Kojak

1 measure Bourbon whiskey
1 measure passion fruit juice
½ measure pineapple juice
1 dash dark rum

Pour all the ingredients into a rocks glass with three cubes of ice. Stir and garnish with a confectioner's lollipop!

La Mamba

1 measure dark rum
½ measure tequila
½ measure blackberry brandy
½ measure Calvados
1 measure apple juice
1 dash Angostura Bitters
Soda to top up

Shake the ingredients well with ice and pour into a large goblet. Top up with soda and float kumquats in the cocktail.

Liberator

1 measure white rum
1 measure Cinzano Rosé
1 dash dry vermouth

Shake the ingredients well with ice and then strain into a cocktail glass. Serve 'straight up' with white flaked almonds floating on top of the cocktail

Mai Tai

½ measure dark rum
1 measure light rum
½ measure tequila
½ measure Triple Sec
½ measure apricot brandy
1 measure orange juice
1 measure pineapple juice
1 dash lemon juice
½ measure grenadine
1 dash Angostura Bitters
½ measure Amaretto or orgeat syrup

Blend all the ingredients with ice until smooth and pour into a hollow pineapple shell. Take slices of fresh lime, pineapple, orange and lemon, also green, orange and red cocktail cherries and spear to the side of the shell with cocktail sticks.

Maracaibo

½ measure amontillado sherry
1 measure white crème de cacao
1 measure dark rum
2 slices of pineapple, roughly chopped
1 measure pineapple juice
1 dash grenadine

Place the ingredients with ice into a blender and blend until smooth. Pour into a brandy balloon garnished with a wedge of pineapple and a maraschino cherry.

Mount Fuji

1½ measures white rum
1½ measures Calvados
½ measure gomme syrup
1 measure lime juice
1 measure apple juice
1 measure Southern Comfort
151° proof rum

Blend all the ingredients, except the 151° proof rum, with a lot of ice to make the cocktail very stiff and then pour into a large goblet. Set into the centre of the goblet half a lime shell filled with 151° proof rum and ignite. A new invention by John Humphries of the London restaurant, Papagallo.

Nassau Night

1 measure De Kuyper Nassau Orange
1 measure dark rum
1 measure Malibu
1 dash lemon juice
1 chopped mango
1 dash Angostura Bitters

Blend all the ingredients with ice until smooth and then pour into a highball glass. Decorate with mango segments and green cherries on sticks.

Maraval

1 measure Malibu
1 measure light rum
1 measure De Kuyper Nassau Orange
½ measure lime juice
1 dash Angostura Bitters

Shake the ingredients well with ice and strain into a cocktail glass. Serve 'straight up'. Decorate with a cherry and a wedge of lime and pineapple pierced by a cocktail stick.

Old Colonial

½ measure Calvados
1 measure Southern Comfort
1 measure dark rum
½ diced paw paw
2 measures mango nectar
2 measures lemon barley water

Shake all the ingredients well with ice and pour into a glass tankard. Decorate with the slices of mango and paw paw on the side of the glass.

Maribou

2 measures light rum
1 measure lemon juice
1 measure Advocaat
½ measure grenadine
1 dash gomme syrup
1 drop grenadine

Blend all the ingredients, except the grenadine, well with ice until smooth. Pour into a wine glass and add a drop of grenadine and then a cherry.

Ocho Rios

1 measure dark rum
1 measure guava juice or nectar
2oz (56g) diced guava
½ measure lime juice

Blend all the ingredients together with ice and then pour into a champagne saucer. Garnish with a maraschino cherry.

Ole Jamaica

1 measure dark rum
1 measure Tia Maria
1 dash Advocaat
1 dash orgeat syrup
1 dash De Kuyper Nassau Orange
1 dash grenadine

Shake the ingredients well with ice and strain into a cocktail glass. Serve straight up with a slice of orange and cherry floating in the cocktail.

Queva

1 measure white rum
1 measure yellow Chartreuse
1 measure apricot brandy
½ measure lime juice
½ measure peach nectar

Shake the ingredients well with ice and then strain into a rocks glass in which a peach has been sliced and arranged back into its original shape.

Riviera

1 measure white rum
½ measure brandy
½ measure framboise
1 dsp whipped cream

Blend all the ingredients with ice and pour into a large goblet. Stir in 2oz (56g) fresh raspberries.

Far left, Springtime (recipe page 66) and then, left to right: Maraval, Mount Fuji, Nassau Night, Springtime, Queva.

Left to right: Solitaire, a bottle of grenadine, Zedd, Tequila Sunrise, Tarantula, Tropicana, V.I.P.

Silk Stockings

1 measure tequila
1 measure white crème de cacao
1 dash apricot whisky
1 measure double cream

Blend the ingredients with ice and when smooth pour into a champagne saucer. Garnish with sliced apricot or peach speared onto a cocktail stick.

Springtime

2 measures white rum
1 measure green crème de menthe
Ginger ale to top up

Place three ice cubes into a highball glass and then pour on the alcohol. Add six black and six green grapes and finally top up the cocktail with ginger ale.

Solitaire

1 measure white rum
1 measure light rum
1 measure orange Curaçao
1 measure lime juice
½ measure orgeat syrup
3 drops orange bitters

Shake the ingredients well with ice and then pour into a large goblet. Top up with soda and decorate the edge of

the glass with the slices of pineapple and orange, a wedge of lime and a maraschino cherry, all speared by a cocktail stick.

Surfside

1 measure light rum
1 measure Southern Comfort
1 measure crème de banane
1 measure peach brandy
1 measure orange juice
1 measure guava nectar
1 dash orgeat syrup
1 dash grenadine

Hollow out a coconut shell leaving approx ¼in (½cm) of flesh inside the shell. Place in a large goblet or bowl filled with crushed ice. Blend all the ingredients with ice until smooth and

Tequila Sunrise

1 measure tequila
Orange juice
1 tsp grenadine

Place ice cubes into a highball glass and add tequila. Pour in orange juice to just below the rim of the glass. Add the grenadine which will sink to the bottom of the glass colouring the orange juice as it does so.

Tropicana

1 measure light rum
½ measure Mandarinette
½ measure orange Curaçao
1 dash lime juice
1 dash Parfait Amour
1 dash Malibu
1 dash lemon juice

Blend with a lot of ice until the mixture is smooth but stiff. Decorate with orange and violet confectioner's flowers on top of the cocktail.

Tropic of Capricorn

1 measure Capricornia
1 measure guava nectar
2 measures Cocoribe
1 measure De Kuyper Nassau Orange
½ measure lemon juice

Blend all the ingredients with ice and then either pour into a large goblet or, if available, a halved coconut shell. Decorate with two pineapple slices pierced by a cocktail stick with a red cherry on one end and a green cherry at the other.

Vesuvius

1 measure white Curaçao
1 egg white
1 dash Anisette
½ measure grapefruit juice
½ measure orange juice
½ measure Galliano

Blend the ingredients together with a lot of ice so that the mixture will be very stiff. Pour into a large goblet. Into the centre of the cocktail place a halved lime shell filled with 151° proof rum and ignite.

V.I.P.

1 measure gin
1 measure Pimms No. 1
2 measures passion fruit juice
½ measure dry vermouth
½ measure lemon juice

Shake the ingredients well together with ice and strain into a cocktail glass. Serve decorated with white water lotus nuts floating in the cocktail.

Zedd

1 measure vodka
1 measure white Curaçao
½ measure Golden Heart
½ measure lemon juice
1 dash grenadine

Shake the ingredients well with ice and then strain into a cocktail glass. Float three lychees in the cocktail.

Zulu

2 measures dark rum
1 chopped mango
1 dash grenadine
1 dash lemon juice
1 dash Pernod
Coco-Cola to top up

Blend the ingredients with ice until smooth and then pour into a large goblet and top up with Coca-Cola. Decorate with a wedge of lime on the side of the glass.

then pour into the coconut shell. Sprinkle with dessicated coconut and place a cherry, speared with a cocktail stick, on the side of the coconut.

Tarantula

1 measure dark rum
1 dash Anisette
1 dash dry vermouth
1 measure pineapple juice
1 measure papaya juice
½ chopped lime
½ chopped mango
1 dash gomme syrup
¼ measure 151° proof rum

Blend all the ingredients with a little ice and pour into a large goblet. Sprinkle with chopped almonds and then float the 151° proof rum on top and ignite.

CREAM COCKTAILS

Thick cream and liqueur – the two main ingredients of these luxurious cream creations. Golden Cadillac, Velvet Hammer, Dizzy Dame – just the names makes them sound expensive, creamy and rich. Not for those on a diet, but irresistible even so, these cream cocktails are so delicious that everyone will want to try one.

The origin of the first cream cocktails is uncertain but their advent was probably around the time of the first egg nogs, milk punches and possets, during the reign of Henry VIII. These cocktails have since evolved into, if not the most delicious, then certainly the richest and sweetest of all cocktails. For those on a diet alcohol in general should be reduced and cream cocktails should really be shunned completely! However, these are the favourite cocktails for many and once tried will always be tempting. Traditionally, cream cocktails were served as an after-dinner cocktail. Considering the texture and taste of most of the cream cocktails this is completely understandable. Nowadays, when so many of the old social taboos are swept aside, almost anything goes, and it is quite acceptable to order a cream cocktail at any time.

The slightest error in over pouring any of the alcoholic ingredients will probably ruin your cocktail. This can prove an extremely expensive business as most of the cream cocktails are made with liqueurs, which are the most expensive items of liquor stock.

The cream should be double cream and not single cream. This will give a nice firm texture to the cocktail whereas single cream tends to make the cocktail taste rather thin.

Cream cocktails should never be pre-mixed, and when you purchase the cream it should be kept in a refrigerator either in the container you have bought it in, or in a glass jug. Never store cream in anything metallic as this will taint the flavour. As cream will sour and deteriorate very quickly

you must be very careful to clean thoroughly all the receptacles you have used for making the cocktail, as any residue of cream left on your equipment will very quickly go bad and contaminate any other cocktails that you may make with this same equipment. If you want to float cream on top of a cocktail or on the top of an Irish Coffee, then ensure that the cream is slightly chilled and that you pour it slowly over the back of a teaspoon or dessertspoon. In the case of an Irish Coffee, if you stir the coffee very gently before adding the cream so that the coffee slowly circulates while the cream is poured on to it, this will create a whorled effect.

Alexander De Kuyper

1 measure De Kuyper Cherry Brandy
1 measure white crème de cacao
1 measure double cream

Shake all the ingredients together well with ice and strain into a champagne saucer. Garnish with two black cherries on a cocktail stick.

Banshee

1 measure crème de banane
1 measure white crème de cacao
1 measure double cream

Shake all the ingredients well with ice and then strain into a cocktail glass with slices of banana floating in the cocktail.

Barbara

1 measure vodka
1 ½ measure white crème de cacao
½ measure double cream

Shake ingredients together with ice and strain into a cocktail glass. Sprinkle a pinch of chocolate vermicelli on to the top of the drink.

The creamy cocktail shown here, Alexander De Kuyper, was invented by the author for De Kuyper Liqueurs.

Camelia

1 measure peach brandy
½ measure brandy
½ measure Triple Sec
½ measure crème de banane
½ measure double cream
2 drops grenadine

Shake all the ingredients, except the grenadine, well with ice and then strain into a champagne goblet. Drop the grenadine into the centre of the cocktail and stir gently three times only anti-clockwise.

Coffee Chaser

½ measure Grand Marnier
½ measure Tia Maria
1 coffee cup black coffee (hot)
2 measures double cream

Place the Grand Marnier and Tia Maria into a large wine goblet and pour in the hot black coffee, stirring while doing so. Float the double cream on to the top by pouring it over a spoon.

Dizzy Dame

1 measure brandy
½ measure Kahlua
½ measure De Kuyper Cherry Brandy
½ measure single cream

Shake the ingredients well with ice and then pour into a rocks glass.

Fernando

1 measure Amaretto
½ measure Chocla Menthe
½ measure Drambuie
1 measure single cream

Shake all the ingredients with ice and strain into a cocktail glass. Stand the glass on a side plate decorated with blanched almonds.

Fifth Avenue

1 measure dark crème de cacao
1 measure orange Curaçao
1 measure double cream

Pour the ingredients into a sherry glass over the back of a teaspoon in the order given.

On the left is shown the small domestic espresso coffee machine now available. The cocktails, left to right, are Dizzy Dame, Fernando, Camelia, Coffee Chaser.

Golden Cadillac

1 measure Triple Sec
1 measure white crème de cacao
½ measure orange juice
2 dashes Galliano
1 measure single cream

Shake the ingredients well with ice and strain into a cocktail glass.

Grasshopper

1 measure green crème de menthe
1 measure white crème de cacao
1 measure double cream

Shake the ingredients with ice and strain into a cocktail glass. Sprinkle a pinch of chocolate vermicelli over the top to garnish. This is one of the most delicious of all the after dinner cocktails.

Jackie K'

1 measure apricot brandy
1 measure Triple Sec
1 measure single cream
1 dash Angostura Bitters
1 drop grenadine

Blend all the ingredients, except the grenadine, with ice until smooth and then pour into a wine glass. Before serving add a drop of grenadine to the top of the cocktail.

Leroy Washington

1 measure brandy
½ measure Tia Maria
½ measure Drambuie
1 measure double cream

Shake the ingredients well with ice, strain into a cocktail glass and serve.

Magnolia Blossom

1 measure gin
1 dash lime juice
1 dash grenadine
1 dash orgeat syrup
1 measure double cream

Shake all the ingredients well with ice and then pour into a rocks glass.

Mandarin

1 measure apricot brandy
½ measure Benedictine
½ measure Galliano
½ measure orange Curaçao
1 measure orange juice
1 measure double cream

Place all the ingredients in a blender with ice until smooth and then pour into a highball glass, adding ice, if necessary, to fill. Garnish with half an apricot resting on the rim of the glass.

Marie Neige

1 measure light rum
½ measure brandy
½ measure Triple Sec
1 dash lime juice
1 dash Parfait Amour
1 measure double cream

Blend together for 30 seconds and then pour into a wine glass and place the cherry to rest over the cocktail pierced with a cocktail stick.

Nassau

1 measure De Kuyper Nassau Orange
½ measure white crème de menthe
½ measure white crème de cacao
1 measure orange juice
1 measure double cream

Blend the ingredients with two cubes of ice until smooth and pour into a wine glass. Garnish with a segment of candied orange fixed to the rim of the glass.

Velvet Hammer

½ measure brandy
½ measure Tia Maria
1 measure Triple Sec
1 measure double cream

Shake the ingredients well with ice and then strain into a cocktail glass.

Widow's Dream

1 egg
1 measure Benedictine
1 measure single cream

Shake the ingredients except the cream together with ice and then pour into a cocktail glass and then carefully float the cream on the top using the back of a teaspoon.

Left to right: Nassau, Golden Cadillac, Widow's Dream, Marie Neige, Mandarin, Grasshopper.

WINE COCKTAILS AND PUNCHES

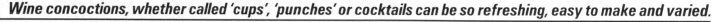

Wine concoctions, whether called 'cups', 'punches' or cocktails can be so refreshing, easy to make and varied.

Here are included cool summer's day Strawberry Fields and Apple Punch as well as

Blenheim and Mantegazza to warm the heart and enliven the spirits.

Although the true cocktail should have a spirit as its base, there are now so many interesting mixed drinks that have wine as a base that those too are now generally referred to as cocktails, though they are more correctly 'cups' or punches.

In the following chapter the wines to be used in the recipes will be stated either as 'dry white wine' or just 'red wine'. In recipes such as these it would be wasteful to use expensive chateau-bottled vintage wines and so it is recommended to use 'vin ordinaire' for the creation of your punches and wine-based cocktails. You may find that in some of the recipes you would like to increase the volume of some of the ingredients to alter the flavour of the drink. If so be extremely careful as you may ruin an expensive creation by the addition of a too strongly-flavoured liquor.

I am sure that most of us at some time have attended punch parties where everyone has brought a bottle of something and during the course of the party each bottle's contents have ended up in the punch, eventually having the most disastrous effects on all

concerned. When inviting friends to a party during which you will be serving punch, ensure that no additions are made to your recipe by your guests.

While preparing hot punches, remember that the boiling point of alcohol is 78°C (172°F) so whatever you do take care never to bring any of the ingredients of the recipes to the temperature for the boiling point of water. It is also better to use an enamel pan rather than an aluminium one as for some reason using an aluminium pan could make your mixture have a bitter taste which no addition of sugar or syrup will remove.

When serving punches with ice in them remember that the ice will melt and dilute the mixture changing the volume and also the flavour. Therefore it is best, unless otherwise stated, to prepare the punches that are to be served cold well in advance. Chill well in a refrigerator and then have an ice bucket at the side of the punch bowl when serving to enable you to add the ice to each drink individually.

Any punch left over from a party may be stored in airtight containers, providing that any fruit has first been removed, preferably by straining the

A cooling punch, Cider Rose, ideal for a hot summer's day but not as innocent as it sounds! (See recipe page 76)

mixture through a fine muslin cloth. If you have any wine left after making up a recipe this will always keep for a few days if it is sealed with a spring-loaded metal top.

Apple Punch

10 glasses
1 measure dark rum
2 measures orange juice
1 measure brandy
2 measures apple juice
1 cinnamon stick
2 cloves
1 pint (56cl) apple cider

Mix all the ingredients together and allow to chill for at least 24 hours in advance of serving, to allow for the flavour of all the ingredients to blend

fully. When serving sprinkle a little grated nutmeg over the top of the glass.

Blenheim

20 glasses
1 bottle Scotch whisky
¼ pint (14cl) orange juice
¼ pint (14cl) water (Malvern)
1 bottle tawny port
6 cloves
2 oranges
1 bottle Apollinaris water

Place all the liquid ingredients except the Apollinaris water into a heavy bottomed cooking pan. Stick three cloves into each of the oranges and place them into the liquor. Bring slowly to the boil and then allow the mixture to simmer for ten minutes. Serve with Apollinaris water added to each glass.

Cider Rose

20 glasses
1 measure Calvados
1 measure brandy
1 measure orange Curaçao
2 pints (approx. 1¼l) apple cider
2 apples
1 measure lemon juice

Slice the apples finely and place in a large jug. Pour on the lemon juice and the remaining liquor and chill for 24 hours before serving.

Ginger Punch

20 glasses
1 bottle dry white wine
¼ pint (14cl) pineapple juice
½ (28cl) pint orange juice
3 dashes Angostura Bitters
1 pint ginger beer

Pour all the ingredients into a large jug and chill for one hour before serving.

Haiti Punch

15 glasses
2 measures De Kuyper Nassau Orange

2 measures brandy
2 measures pineapple juice
1 bottle dry white wine
½ pint (28cl) of soda water to serve

Mix all the ingredients well and chill well. On serving add the soda water and pour into goblets.

Honey-Bun

20 glasses
2 pints (approx. 1¼l) water
½ bottle gin
1lb Mexican clear honey
4 measures orange juice
4 measures lemon juice
4 cloves
1 stick cinnamon

Dissolve the honey in the hot water and then add the other ingredients and bring all the liquor to the boil. Remove from the heat and extract the cinnamon stick. Chill for 24 hours at least, before serving.

Inigo Jones

1 glass
1 measure Marsala
1 measure brandy
1 measure Cinzano Rosé
1 dash lemon juice
1 dash orange juice

Mix the ingredients with ice and then strain into a rocks glass, half-filled with crushed ice with a twist of orange peel resting on the top.

Jerez

1 glass
1 measure amontillado sherry
1 measure peach brandy
1 measure dry white wine
1 dash Angostura Bitters
1 dash Prunelle

Pour the ingredients into a mixing glass with three cubes of ice and mix well until chilled. Pour into a rocks glass and serve. This recipe is purported to be an old Spanish recipe from one of the noble houses of Spain.

Lulu

1 glass
1 measure Scotch whisky
½ measure orange Curaçao
1 dash lemon juice
1 dash orange juice
1 dash Angostura Bitters
Coca-Cola to top up

Shake all the ingredients, except the Coca-Cola, well with ice. Pour into a highball glass which contains a wedge of lemon and top up the drink with the Coca-Cola.

Mitre

1 glass
2 measures of heavy red wine
1 measure orange juice
1 dash lemon juice
1 dash gomme syrup
Ginger ale to top up

Shake all the ingredients, except the ginger ale, well with ice and then pour into a large wine goblet. Finally top up with the ginger ale. This cocktail is believed to have been created by a curate at Winchester Cathedral, for his Bishop.

Montcalm

15 glasses
1 measure light rum
1 measure brandy
1 measure Benedictine
1 measure peach brandy
2 pints (approx. 1¼l) apple cider

Chill the ingredients well by placing in a jug in a refrigerator until well chilled, and then serve.

Left to right: Cider Rose, Haiti Punch, Jerez, Mitre, and a bottle of Martini Rosé.

77

Mantegazza

10 glasses
¼ bottle De Kuyper Cherry Brandy
¼ bottle De Kuyper Nassau Orange
1 bottle Lambrusco
2lb (1kg approx) black cherries
2 lemons chopped into a fine dice

Stone the cherries and soak overnight in a mixture of the De Kuyper Cherry Brandy, Nassau Orange and chopped lemons. The following day, before serving, heat the red wine until just below boiling point and then pour over the fruit and liqueurs. Serve hot.

Pennsylvania

15 glasses
1 measure peach brandy
1 measure Bourbon whiskey
1 measure brandy
1 measure Southern Comfort
1 bottle Californian red wine
1 pint (56cl) ginger ale
2 chopped apricots
2 chopped peaches

Place all the ingredients including the ginger ale into a large bowl with the apricots and peaches. Chill for 24 hours before serving.

Somerset

25 glasses
2 pints (approx 1½l) apple cider
¼ bottle fine sherry
¼ pint (14cl) orange juice
¼ pint (14cl) lemon juice
3 dashes Angostura Bitters
2 sprigs of mint
Rind of 1 cucumber

Chop the mint and cucumber roughly and steep in the sherry, bitters and juices for 24 hours. Strain through fine muslin and add the cider. Chill for a further 24 hours before serving.

Strawberry Fields

20 glasses
1 bottle dry white wine
1 bottle Anjou rosé
½ bottle brandy
1lb (450g) strawberries
1 dash lemon juice
2oz (56g) caster sugar
2 measures fraise

Clean the strawberries and cover with the caster sugar and the dash of lemon juice. Leave for six hours. Add brandy and wine and leave in a refrigerator to chill for at least 18 hours before serving.

St. Charles

10 glasses
2 measures brandy
2 measures Triple Sec
1 measure ruby port
1 measure lemon juice
1 dash gomme
1 bottle dry white wine

Mix all the ingredients together in a large punch bowl or glass jug and chill well before serving.

Taronga Twist

20 glasses
1 bottle sweet Australian sherry
¼ bottle brandy
¼ bottle apricot brandy
¼ pint (14cl) grapefruit juice
¼ pint (14cl) water
3 slices of roughly chopped fresh pineapple

Boil sherry and brandy together and then add the other liquor and simmer for 15 minutes. Add the pineapple to the mixture, allow to cool and then chill for six hours before serving.

Tea Punch

1 glass
1 measure dark rum
½ measure brandy
1 dash lemon juice
1 dash gomme
1 dash Angostura Bitters
1 cup hot green tea

Shake all the other ingredients together, except for the tea. Pour them into a highball glass and add the hot tea. This is an old Bostonian recipe and can be slightly altered so that, after having added the tea, the whole drink may be chilled and served as a very refreshing beverage with crushed ice.

The General

40 glasses
1 bottle good claret
1 bottle champagne 'Brut'
½ pint (28cl) soda water
½ bottle brandy
½ bottle orange Curaçao

Chill all the ingredients well before mixing and then only mix just before

serving. This old army recipe also states 'a tankard of porter may be added to give more body'!

Twister

1 glass
1 measure dry sherry
1 measure orange juice
½ measure Scotch whisky
1 dash Triple Sec
White wine (dry) to top up

Mix all the ingredients except the white wine together and pour into a long glass with a little crushed ice and top up with white wine. Garnish with twists of orange and lemon peel.

Left to right: Mantegazza, Strawberry Fields, Somerset, Lulu (recipe page 77), The General.

CHAMPAGNE COCKTAILS

Champagne cocktails – the most luxurious of them all, to add a touch of fantasy to any occasion – or, indeed, because it is so special, to create an occasion in its own right.

The 'wine of kings and the king of wines' is how this wonderful wine has been described. There is probably no better description for champagne, recognized throughout the world as the only drink to celebrate with.

Although there are other French sparkling wines, true champagne comes from the region of France surrounding the towns of Epernay and Reims and was originally introduced to the area by the Romans at the start of the third century. The vines were then cultivated by the various religious orders in that area. Around the fourteenth century this wine was offered to the kings of France, who came to be crowned in the cathedral of Reims.

Towards the end of the seventeenth century the method of bottling the wine at the right time to make it retain its pale colour and sparkling qualities was discovered.

Although the many champagne cocktail recipes in this book specify champagne, a sparkling wine may be used instead, such as Kriter or Cinzano Sparkling Wine. It should be noted that there are many inferior types which could easily ruin a cocktail. Therefore, for any recipes which recommend using champagne, whenever possible, it is advisable to use a good dry (Brut) champagne. Ideally, try to aim always to keep a few bottles of champagne in reserve. After all, this is the drink that is recognized universally as the ultimate in elegance and luxury and therefore why not use and enjoy it to create many more special occasions!

Champagne can be bought in varying sizes of bottles from the 'split', which is a quarter bottle, to a Nebuchadnezzar, which is 20 times the normal size. Most suitable for the refrigerator is the standard bottle.

The classic glass to serve champagne in is not, as is so often believed, the champagne saucer, but a champagne flute, which is designed to withhold the effervescence.

There are several stories about how and when the champagne cocktail came into being, but a popular view is that a prominent member of the English court in the late nineteenth century was the first to discover it delights. The trick of serving a good champagne cocktail is to ensure that all the liquid ingredients have been well-chilled before making up the drink.

The Classic Champagne Cocktail is
shown here with a swizzle stick.
(See recipe page 85)

Ajaccio

½ measure gin
½ measure grapefruit juice
1 dash Anisette
Champagne to top

Shake the gin, Anisette and grapefruit juice well with ice. Strain into a champagne saucer half-filled with crushed ice and with two crystallized confectioner's violets on top of the crushed ice.

Alfonso

1 measure Dubonnet
1 dash lemon juice
1 dash Angostura Bitters
1 dash gomme
Champagne to top

Half fill a highball glass with ice and add the Dubonnet, juice and bitters with the gomme. Mix together, then add the champagne to fill the glass. Rest a carnation on the side of the glass.

Left, Champagne Cooler with a bottle of Taittinger champagne. Right, Barracuda, Bellini, Alfonso, Aquilas.

Aquilas

½ measure Spanish brandy
½ measure Grand Marnier
½ measure Orange Curaçao
½ measure Maraschino
Spanish sparkling wine to top

Stir the spirits well together and then pour onto a goblet half filled with crushed ice. Top up with the champagne. Place a garnish of a cocktail stick piercing an orange slice and two black grapes over the top of the glass. This cocktail originated in the cocktail bar of Hotel Los Aquilas in Tenerife.

Barracuda

1 measure light rum
½ measure Galliano
1 measure pineapple juice
1 dash lime juice
Champagne to top

Shake all the ingredients, except the champagne, and then pour into a large goblet filled with shaved ice. Top up with the champagne and float red rose petals on the top of the drink.

Bellini

3 measures peach nectar
Champagne to top
1 fresh peach

Place three slices of peach that have been soaked in lemon juice and brandy overnight into the bottom of a wine goblet. Pour on the brandy, followed by the champagne which should be well chilled.

Black Velvet

¼ pint (14cl) Guinness (preferably draught)
¼ pint (14cl) very dry champagne

Into a glass tankard pour the Guinness followed by the champagne. This is one of the most famous of drinks with champagne and dates back to the nineteenth century.

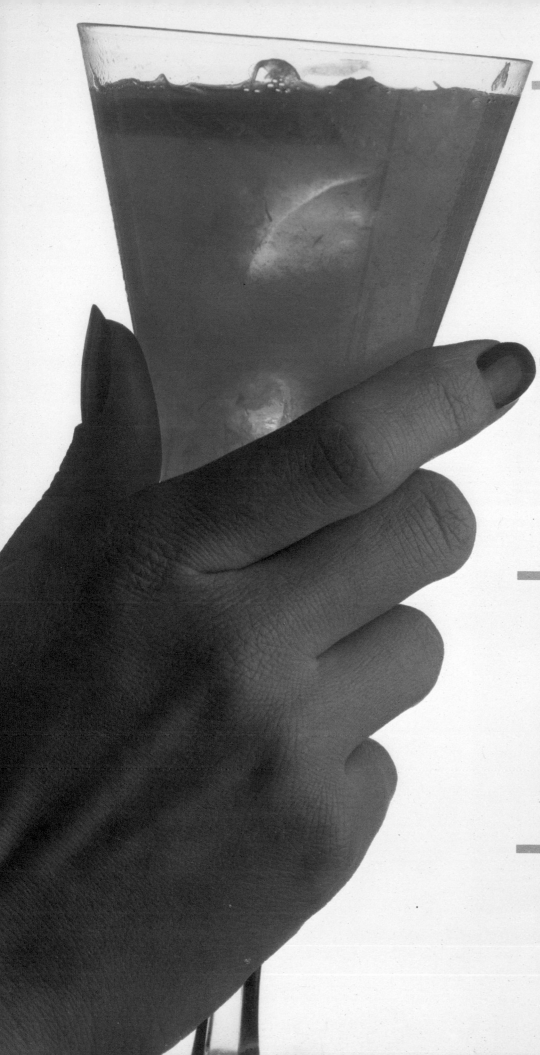

Buck's Fizz

Orange juice
Champagne

Yet another famous drink with champagne. Although there seem to be no hard and fast rules on the preparation of this it is advisable to use freshly-made orange juice and to use a good quality dry champagne. Take a ratio per person of three parts of orange juice to five parts champagne. Ice should not be put into a Buck's Fizz but the ingredients and glass should be well chilled.

Camp Champ

1 measure Campari
½ measure orange juice
Champagne to top

Mix the Campari and orange juice together in a highball glass and then add three cubes of ice. Top up with the champagne and decorate with a slice of orange and a cherry which have been speared by a cocktail stick.

Champagne Cooler

1 measure De Kuyper Nassau Orange
½ measure brandy
1 dash orange bitters
Champagne to top

Fill a highball glass with crushed ice and then add orange bitters and Nassau Orange liqueur. Top this with champagne and decorate with thin strips of cucumber rind running up the inside of the glass with the ends just above the top of the glass. Place confectioner's flowers to rest on the ends of the cucumber stalks.

Champness

½ measure port
½ measure dark rum
1 dash Triple Sec
4in (10cm) cucumber (approx size)
Champagne to top

Hollow out the cucumber and fit it into

the highball glass so that it is just over the rim of the glass. Pour in the port, rum and Triple Sec and chill for two to three hours. Top up with champagne and serve.

Champoo

¼ measure Amaretto
¼ measure orange Curaçao
1 dash lemon juice
Champagne to top

Place the Amaretto, Curaçao and lemon juice into a champagne saucer and fill up with the champagne. Add a twist of orange.

Classic Champagne Cocktail

1 lump of sugar
2 dashes Angostura Bitters
1 measure brandy
Champagne

Place the sugar lump into the bottom of a champagne flute or wine glass and shake on the Angostura Bitters. Add the brandy and finally the champagne. A suggested garnish, although not obligatory, is to float a slice of orange on top of the cocktail.

Left, Buck's Fizz. Right, Buck's Fizz, Black Velvet (recipe page 83), Champness, Perrier Jouet champagne.

Left to right: Champagne pliers, a bottle of Taittinger champagne, Jubilee, Emerald Sparkler, Mark Hopkins, Lovett, Ojos Verdes, Kir.

Emerald Sparkler

1 measure Midori
Champagne to top up

Pour the Midori into a champagne saucer and then top up with dry champagne. Garnish with a maraschino cherry on a cocktail stick, or a parasol.

Happy Youth

½ measure De Kuyper Cherry Brandy
1 sugar lump
½ measure brandy
Champagne to top

Make as for the Classic Champagne Cocktail but garnish with three black cherries floating in the cocktail.

Jubilee

1 measure Sloe gin
1 dash Triple Sec
1 dash lemon juice
1 dash Angostura Bitters
Champagne to top

Shake all the ingredients together with ice, except the champagne, and then strain into a long glass filled with crushed ice. Top up with the champagne and decorate with a rose bud on top of the glass. A wonderful way to help 'someone special' start the day.

Kir

½ measure crème de cassis
Champagne

Pour the champagne into a champagne flute and then add the crème de cassis. This is a classic champagne cocktail which goes back for many years. If preferred a dry white wine may be substituted for the champagne and a sprig of blackcurrants (when in season) hung over the edge of the glass.

Lovett

½ measure pure redcurrant juice
½ measure pure apple juice
Champagne to top

Fill a champagne flute or long glass with crushed ice and then pour in the juices. Top up with the champagne and finally add a twist of lemon.

Mark Hopkins

½ measure brandy
½ measure Triple Sec
1 dash Mandarinette
1 dash Maraschino
1 dash pineapple juice
Champagne

Mix all the ingredients except the champagne with ice and pour into a tall glass, which contains pineapple and mandarin segments in the base and is half-filled with crushed ice. Top up with the champagne. This cocktail is said to have been invented for the founder of the famous hotel of the same name in San Francisco.

Maxims

½ measure brandy
½ measure Cointreau
½ measure orange juice
1 dash framboise
Champagne to top

Mix the brandy, Cointreau and orange juice with ice and then strain into a champagne saucer. Pour on the champagne and finally add a dash of framboise. This was created especially for the famous Parisienne restaurant of the same name.

Ojos Verdes

1 measure Midori
½ measure Fundador Spanish Brandy
1 dash Angostura Bitters
Spanish sparkling wine to top up

Shake the Midori, Fundador and Bitters together and pour into a wine goblet that has been half filled with crushed ice. Top up with sparkling wine.

More popular than ever nowadays, cocktails or 'mocktails' without alcohol can be just as tantalizing and 'out of this world' to look at and taste as some of their alcoholic equivalents. Be inventive and use the many new sodas, fruit syrups and juices now available with care and as much devotion as you would for a spirit-based drink.

With the continuing cult for healthy living, exercise studios and health foods, many would-be imbibers of alcoholic cocktails have taken to drinking 'mocktails' — which can taste as delicious and look as exciting as any of the alcoholic concoctions. Non-alcoholic cocktails are ideal also for children's parties, for the diet conscious, friends who simply do not like alcohol and, of course, those suffering from the effects of the night before.

Although only a few recipes are shown here, it is extremely simple to concoct your own mocktails, using some of the wide range of juices, nectars, sodas and syrups available today.

Beach Baby

6fl oz (17cl) full cream milk
1 dsp Mexican honey
1 scoop vanilla ice cream
½ banana

Blend all the ingredients together until smooth and then pour into a large goblet.

Belle Star

2 measures blueberry juice
¼ measure lemon juice
1 dash Angostura Bitters
1 small bottle ginger ale

Shake the juices and Bitters together with ice and then pour into a highball glass and top up with ginger ale. This was believed to be a drink created for the famous American saloon owner of the same name.

Bullrushes

¾ measure lemon juice
1 dash Tabasco Sauce
1 dash Worcestershire Sauce
½ pint cold consommé
¼ pint tomato juice
seasoning

Fill a large goblet half with consommé and half tomato juice and add the other ingredients. Pour into a cocktail shaker with ice. Shake well and pour back into the goblet. Decorate with a stick of celery to stir the drink.

Campbells

1 bottle lemonade
1 dash Angostura Bitters
1 dash orgeat

To a large glass of lemonade on the rocks add the Angostura Bitters and orgeat syrup. Stir gently in order not to lose the colour of the cordials.

For delicious non-alcoholic cocktails take advantage of the many syrups now available. Here, grenadine and orgeat syrup are being used to make San Francisco. (See recipe page 91)

Lamb's Passion

1 measure pineapple juice
1 measure orange juice
½ measure passion fruit juice
1 dash fraise (syrup)
1 dash orgeat
1 egg white

Blend all the ingredients together with ice until smooth and then pour into a rocks glass. Decorate with a twist of orange on the side.

Limey

1 measure lime juice
½ measure lemon juice
1 egg white
1 dash gomme syrup

Shake all the ingredients well together with ice and then strain into a cocktail glass garnishing with a maraschino cherry on a stick.

Margaret Rose

4 strawberries
1 slice chopped pineapple
1 dash lime juice
1 dash guava nectar
2 dashes fraise syrup
Soda to top up

Blend all the ingredients, except the soda, together with ice until smooth. Pour into a goblet and top up with the soda. Decorate with fresh strawberries and pineapple segments arranged on the side of the glass.

Mary Jane

¼ measure lime juice
½ measure orange juice
1 bottle bitter lemon
1 dash Angostura Bitters

Fill a large goblet with crushed ice and pour in the bitters and fruit juices followed by the bitter lemon. Garnish with a wedge of lime and maraschino cherry speared together on a cocktail stick.

and the pour into a goblet or highball glass and top up with the lemonade. This was created for one of Walt Disney's child stars whom he discovered in England.

Greyhound

4 measures grapefruit juice
1 dash Angostura Bitters
Salt

Rim a rocks glass with the salt (see garnishes p 28) add three ice cubes, the Bitters and finally the grapefruit juice, making sure that the liquor does not touch the rim.

Inca Gold

4 measure pineapple juice
1 measure grapefruit juice
2 measures coconut cream
1 measure single cream
2 drops of grenadine

Blend all the ingredients with ice until smooth and then pour into a highball glass, add the grenadine and set a segment of pineapple on the side of the glass.

Jersey

1 small bottle non-alcoholic cider
2 dashes grenadine

Pour the ingredients into a wine glass with a little crushed ice and decorate with a slice of cucumber and a cherry.

Cindy O'

½ measure lemon juice
1 measure lime juice
½ measure pineapple juice
1 measure peach nectar
1 dash orgeat
1 dash grenadine
Lemonade to top up

Shake all the ingredients well with ice

Morning Glory

1 small can oyster juice
6fl oz (17cl) tomato juice
6fl oz (17cl) celery root juice
black pepper to season

Stir all the ingredients well with ice and then pour into a highball glass. Serve with melba toast.

New England

2 measures clam juice
2 measures tomato juice
1 dash Worcestershire sauce
1 dash Tabasco sauce
1 dash Angostura Bitters
1 egg

Shake all the ingredients well together with ice and pour into a goblet or highball glass. Decorated with either a stick of celery or, for the little more adventurous, lemon grass, which will impart a little extra flavour to the recipe.

Papillon

1 measure orgeat
1 measure fraise syrup
1 diced mango
2 measures mango nectar
1 measure pineapple juice

Blend all the ingredients together with ice until smooth and then pour them into a large goblet which has been decorated with slices of pineapple dipped in grenadine to resemble butterfly wings.

R.C.

3 cubes redcurrant jelly
2 tbs of water
2 measures lemon juice
Lemonade to top up

Dissolve the jelly in the water and lemon juice over a low heat and then allow to cool slightly. Pour into a highball glass over ice. Top up with the lemonade and garnish with a long twist of lemon peel on top of the drink.

Sally Anne

1 measure unsweetened redcurrant juice
1 scoop Italian vanilla ice cream
1 dash menthe cordial or syrup
Soda to top up

Pour the redcurrant juice over the ice cream which should be in a large goblet, top up with the soda and finally add the menthe. An afternoon favourite at the International Bar in Venice.

San Francisco

1 measure orange juice
½ measure lemon juice
1 measure pineapple juice
1 measure grapefruit juice
1 egg white
1 dash grenadine

Shake all the ingredients well together with ice and then pour into a large goblet or tankard and top up with soda. Garnish with a selection of fruit segments on the rim of the glass.

Shenley Lodge

1 egg
1 banana
1 tbs of yoghurt (live)
1 dsp Mexican honey
1 tsp wheatgerm
1 tsp lecithin
6fl oz (17cl) goat's milk
1 chopped mango

Blend all the ingredients, except the mango, for one minute. Pour into a glass tankard. Add the chopped mango.

Left to right: Lamb's Passion, Inca Gold, Cindy O', Margaret Rose

Temperance

2 egg yolks
2 measures lemon juice
2 measures grenadine

Shake the ingredients with ice and strain in to a cocktail glass.

Ugly Bug

1 measure orange juice
1 measure grapefruit juice
1 measure pineapple juice
1 measure prune juice

Mix the juice together in a jug or glass and place in a refrigerator until well chilled. Serve in a goblet.

Waabine Cooler

2 dashes Angostura Bitters
1 measure lime juice
1 small bottle ginger beer

Mix the lime juice and Angostura Bitters in a highball glass and add three cubes of ice and a wedge of lemon or lime and then top up with ginger beer. This is an old Trinidadian recipe — Waabine is a Trinidadian expression of endearment.

Yellow Dwarf

1 measure orgeat
1 measure single cream
1 egg yolk

Shake the ingredients together with ice and then strain into a champagne saucer, finally decorating with a maraschino cherry on a stick.

Zibi

1 measure mango nectar
1 measure coconut cream
1 dash lime juice
1 measure pineapple juice
1 dash grenadine (to garnish)

Blend all the ingredients together with ice until smooth and pour into a wine glass. Add the dash of grenadine to the top of the finished cocktail and decorate the glass with a slice or wedge of pineapple on the side.

Left, Ugly Bug, Yellow Dwarf, Shenley Lodge (recipe page 91), Zibi. Right, an Alka Seltzer tablet being dissolved in water.

THE MORNING AFTER

There is no reason for the morning after to be terrible and the memories of those delicious fantasies to be just a headache. Take care how and what and, needless to say, how much you drink, but if you do wake up the morning after feeling the worse for wear, try some of the following remedies.

Life's cares are a poison and alcohol it's best antidote.' Whether as a result of a temporary escape from the cares of life, celebrating a happy event or just getting together with friends, we've all woken up on some morning during our lives and sworn 'never again'. How long that 'never again' hangover actually lasts is a matter of conjecture but usually this period lasts between 6 and 24 hours. What is a hangover? Well, a hangover is a deficiency of oxygen in the blood stream and dehydration caused by the intake of too much alcohol. Possibly the most natural cure for a hangover, when you eventually wake up, is to take several deep breaths in front of an open window, drink a pint of cold water and go back to bed and back to sleep, letting your body take over with it's natural healing process. For some of us this can be a couple of hours and for others, unfortunately, it can mean suffering for the rest of the day. There are various theories on how best to avoid a hangover and all seem agreed that you should never drink alcohol on an empty stomach. The ideal preventative is to eat a light meal before you go out, or if you can't find the time then a pint of milk or a tablespoon of olive oil are also said to be good preventatives.

When you are drinking try to avoid mixing your drinks. If you really do want to avoid having a hangover then if you are a spirit drinker stay with that and have only either water or ice with your drink. This may not seem a very enthralling prospect knowing the other many more exciting possibilities, unless you are a Scotch on the Rocks or Scotch and Water imbiber. Many of you will have attended dinner parties where your host has served cocktails, then two or three wines throughout dinner, followed by either after-dinner cocktails, liqueurs or port. Unless you really want to risk a bad hangover you will have to make up your mind to drink only wine for the evening and drink soft drinks before and after the meal, or at least do try and drink in moderation. You will be lucky if your host makes a brandy-based cocktail before the meal and then offers a brandy or a brandy-based cocktail afterwards. Drinking plenty of black coffee at the end of the evening will probably have no effect on your hangover at all. In fact, you'll probably feel worse as the coffee will keep you awake. When you get home from your evening's revelry drink two pints of cold water slowly and take two aspirins.

For those of you that are a little har-dier the following two recipes may just shock your system back to normality:

Hair of the Dog

2 measure Scotch whisky
1½ measure double cream
1 measure clear honey

Shake the ingredients well with crushed ice and pour into a rocks glass.

The Invigorator

1 egg
½ tea cup of strong cold black coffee
1 measure brandy
1 measure port
sugar

Shake the egg by itself in the shaker until well mixed then add the other ingredients with sugar to taste

If you've managed to get half way through the day and are still feeling a little muzzy at lunchtime the best idea is to find a friend and split a bottle of champagne so that the final haze of your hangover fades into oblivion — until the next time!

Two cocktails to help a hangover, Invigorator and Hair of the Dog.

INDEX

The page numbers indicated in bold refer to photographs:

Absinthe 44
Advocaat 10
Ajaccio 83
Alexander De Kuyper 68, **69**
Alfonso 83, **83**
Alka Seltzer **93**
Almond Syrup 10
Amaretto 10
Americano 14, **15**
Andante 46
Angostura Bitters 10, 14, **47**
Anisette 10
Aperitif glass **26**
Applejack 10
Apple Punch 76
Après-Midori 46
Apricot Brandy 10
Apricot Lady **59**, 60
Apricot Sour 42
Aquilas **37**, 83, **83**
Arak 8
Armagnac 10
Arthur's Day Dream 10, **10**
Arthur's, Sydney 10

Bacardi 10, **17**
Bachanal 60
Bananas (Crème de) 10
Banshee 68
Barbara 68
Barracuda 83, **83**
Bar, Stocking of 14-17
Beach Baby 88
Belle Star 88
Bellini 83, **83**
Benedict Arnold 46
Benedictine 10
Betsy Ross 46
Between the Sheets 42, **43**
Blackberry Brandy 10
Black Forest 47
Black Velvet 83, **85**
Bleeding Heart 47, **47**
Blender 18, **19**, **21**, 32
Blending 32
Blenheim 76
Bloody Mary 43, **43**
Blue Hawaii 60, **60**
Bottle brush 20
Bottle opener 16, 20
Bottle seals 20
Bourbon 10
Brandy 10, 14, 44, 58
Brandy-based Cocktails
    Apple Punch 76
    Aquilas **37**, 83, **83**
    Betsy Ross 46
    Between the Sheets 42, **43**
    Black Forest 83, **85**
    Camelia 71, **71**
    Champagne Cooler **82**, 84
    Champs Élysée **47**, 49
    Chicago 49, **49**
    Cider Rose **75**, 76, **77**
    Claridges **47**, 49

Classic Champagne Cocktail **37**, **81**, 85
Dizzy Dame 71, **71**
Foxhouse 50, **50**
Haiti Punch 76, **77**
Happy Youth 87
Inigo Jones 77
Invigorator, The 94, **94**
Leroy Washington 72
Marie Neige 72, **73**
Mark Hopkins **86**, 87
Maxims 87
Montcalm 77
Ojos Verdes **86**, 87
Pennsylvania 78
Riviera 65
Sidecar 42
St. Charles 78
Stinger 42, **43**
Strawberry Fields 78, **79**
Taronga Twist 78
Tea Punch 78
Vanderbilt 57, **57**
Velvet Hammer 72
Washington 57
Brandy balloon glass 24
Brandy, Apricot 10
    Blackberry 10
    Cherry 11
    Peach 11
Brooklyn 47, **47**
Buck's Fizz 84, **84**
Bullrushes 88
Bullshot 43

Cacao (Crème de) 10, 14
Calvados 10
Calypso 61
Camelia 71, **71**
Campari 10, 14, **17**
Campbells 88
Camp Champ **37**, 84
Canada 47
Candide 47
Capricornia 10
Caracas 61, **61**
Cascade 61, **61**
Cassis (Crème de) 11
Champagne 8, 11, 80, 94
Champagne bucket 20
Champagne Cocktails 80-87
Champagne Cooler **82**, 84
Champagne glasses, flute 24, **24-26**, 80
    saucer 24, **26**, **41**, 80
Champagne pliers 21, **86**
Champness 84, **85**
Champoo 85
Champs Elysée **47**, 49
Chartreuse 11
Cherry Brandy 11, 14, **15**, **16-17**
Chicago 49, **49**
Chichirera **44-45**, 47, 49
Chocla Menthe 11
Cider 11
Cider Rose **75**, 76, **77**
Cincher **48**, 49
Cindy O' 90, **91**
Claridges **47**, 49
Classic Champagne Cocktail **37**, **81**, 85
Classic Cocktails 40-43
Cloths 21, 24
Cocktail glass 24, **27**
Cocktail party 36, 37
Cocktail shaker 16, 21, **21**, **23**
Cocoriba 11
Coffee Chaser 71, **71**
Coffee machine 21, **70-71**
Cognac 11, **17**
Cointreau 11, 14

Collins 42
Collins glass 26
Colonial Boy 47, 49
Conchita 61
Corcovado 61
Corkscrew 21
Cream cocktail glass **26**
Cream cocktails 68-73
Crème de Bananes 10
Crème de Cacao 10, 14
Crème de Cassis 11
Crème de Menthe 11
'Cups' 74
Curaçao 11

Daquiri 42, **43**, 61
Darlajane 49, **49**
Dash bottle 22
Dispensers 22
Dizzy Dame 71, **71**
Drambuie 11
Dubonnet 11
Dunhill **48**, 49
Dusky Maiden 61

Egril 61
Embassy Royale 50
Emerald Sparkler **86**, 87
Etonian 50
Equipment 16, 18-23

Fernando 71, **71**
Fernet Branca 11
Fifth Avenue 71
Fine and Dandy 50
Flaming **34**, 35
Floating 35
Food to accompany cocktails **36**, 37
Forbidden Fruit 11
Foxhound 50, **50**
Fraise 11
Framboise 11
Frosting 28
Frozen Fruit Daquiri 61
Fruit Cocktail Glass 26
Fruit Cocktails 58-67
Fruit juices 14
Fruit peeler **21**
Fruit sours 42
Fruit squeezer **21**, 23

Galliano 11, **51**
Garnishes 28-31, **29**, **30-31**
Geisha 61, 62
General, The 78, **79**
Genever 11
Gibson Martini 28, **35**, 36, 40, **41**
Gin 11, 14, 44
Gin-based Cocktails
    Ajaccio 83
    Andante 46
    Candide 47
    Caracas 61, **61**
    Cascade 61, **61**
    Cincher **48**, 49
    Darlajane 49, **49**
    Dunhill **48**, 49
    Etonian 50
    Fine and Dandy 50
    Honey-Bun 77
    Hong Kong Fizz 50
    Jubilee **86**, 87
    Magnolia Blossom 72
    Martini 11, 14, 28, **35**, 36, 40, 44
    Millionaire 53
    Negroni 53
    Pall Mall 54
    R.A.C. 54
    Ramos Fizz 6, **6**

Red Lion 55
Rosé Glow 55
Sakini 54, **56**
Shanghai Gin Fizz 56
Sixty-Six 56
Skyline 56, **57**
V.I.P. **66**, 67
Wedding Bells 57
Ginger Punch 76
Glasses 24-27, **26-27**
Golden Cadillac 72, **73**
Golden Heart 11, 14, **47**
Gomme syrup 11, 14
Grand Marnier 11
Grasshopper 72, **73**
Green Widow **48**, 50
Grenadine 11, 14, **66**, 89
Greyhound 90

Hair of the Dog 94, **94**
Haitian Gold **61**, 62
Haiti Punch 76, **77**
Hangover cures 93-94
Hannibal Palace 62, **62**
Happy Youth 87
Harlequin 63
Harvey Wallbanger 35, 50, **51**
Hawthorne strainer **20**, 23
Highball glass 26, **27**
Hiroshima 50, **51**
Hoffman glass 26
Honey-Bun 77
Honeymoon 50
Hong Kong Fizz 50

ice 16, **18**, 74
Ice bowl 23
Ice bucket 16, 23, **23**, 74
Ice tongs 23, 23
Ice crusher 23
Iced tea 7, **7**
Ice scoop 23, **23**
Ice tray 23
Inca Gold 90, **91**
Inigo Jones 77
Invigorator 94, **94**
Irish Whiskey 11

Jackie K 72
Jade 50, **51**
Jerez 77, **77**
Jersey 90
Jigger 23
Jubilee **86**, 87
Jug 23, **23**
Julia **62**, 63

Kahlua 11
Katinka 51
Kava 8
King prawns **36**
Kir **86**, 87
Kirsch 11
Kojak 62, 63
Krakatao 6, **6**
Kummel 11

Ladle 23
La Mamba **62**, 63
Lamb's Passion 90, **91**
Lark 51
Layering 35
Leroy Washington 72
Liberator 63
Lillet 11
Liqueur glass **21**, 26
Limey 90
Liquidizer 18, 23
L'Opéra 52, **52**
Lovett **86**, 87
Lulu 77, **79**

Madeira 11
Magnolia Blossom 72
Mai Tai **62**, 63
Mallet 23
Mandarin 72, **73**
Mandarinette 11
Manhattan 40, 44
Mantegazza 78, **79**
Maracaibo 63
Maraschino 11
Maraschino cherry **29**, 30
Maraval 64, **65**
Margaret Rose 90, **91**
Margarita 28, 42
Maribou 64
Marie Neige 72, **73**
Marijka 52, **52**
Mark Hopkins **86**, 87
Marsala 11
Martini 11, 14, 28, **35**, 36, 40, 44
Martini Glass **25**
Martini Rosé **77**
Mary Jane 90
Maxims 87
Measures 16, 23, **23**, 40
Melon Driver 52
Menthe (Crème de) 11
Metaxa 11
Mexican Melon 53
Midori 11, 14
Midori Sour 53, **53**
Midori Tropical 53, **54**
Millionaire 53
Millionairess **51**, 53
Mint Julep 32, **52**, 53
Mitre 77, **77**
Mixing 32
Mixing Beaker **23**
  Glass 23
  Jar 23
  Jug 16, 23
  Spoon 16, 23
Mocktails 88
Montcalm 77
Morning Glory 91
Moscow Melon 53, **54**
Moscow Mule 53, **54**
Mount Fuji 64, **65**
Muddling 32
Muddling spoon 16, 23, **23, 34, 35**

Nassau 72, **72**
Nassau Night 64, **65**
Nassau Orange 11
Negroni 53
New England 91
New Orleans Punch 9, **9**
Noilly Prat 11, 40
Non-alcoholic cocktails 88-92

Oblomow Bar, Amsterdam 6
O Cha 11
Ocho Rios 64
Off the Rails 53
Ojos Verdes **86**, 87
Okinawa Sunrise **52**, 54
Old Colonial 64
Old Fashioned 32, 40
Ole Jamaica 65
'On the Rocks' 36
Orgeat 11, **89**
Ouzo 11

Pall Mall 54
Papillon 91
Parfait Amour 11
Parrot 54, **54**
Party, Cocktail 36
Pastis 11
Peach Brandy 11
Pennsylvania 78

Pernod 11
Persico 11
Pilsner glass 26, **27**
Pink Almond 54
Pitcher 23
Port 11
Port glass 26
Pourer **18**, 22
Pouring 35, **68**
Pousse Café **33**, 35
Punch bowl 23
Punches 74-79

Queva 65, **65**

R.A.C. 54
R.C. 91
Ramos Fizz 6, **6**
Red Lion 55
Reids Flip 55
Rimming 28
Riviera 65
Rob Roy 14, **15**, 40
Rocks glass 26, **26, 27**
Rosé Glow 55
Royale **54**, 55
Rum 11, 14, 44, 58
Rum-based Cocktails
  Apple Punch 76
  Apricot Lady **59**, 60
  Bachanal 60
  Between the Sheets 42, **43**
  Blue Hawaii 60, **60**
  Calypso 61
  Champness 84, **85**
  Dusky Maiden 61
  Egrit 61
  Frozen Fruit Daquiri 61
  Haitian Gold **61**, 62
  Harlequin 63
  Jade 50, **51**
  Julia **62**, 63
  La Mamba **62**, 63
  L'Opéra 52, **52**
  Liberator 63
  Mai Tai 62, 63
  Maracaibo 63
  Maraval 64, **65**
  Maribou 64
  Marie Neige 72, **73**
  Millionairess **51**, 53
  Montcalm 77
  Mount Fuji 64, **65**
  Nassau Night 64, **65**
  Ocho Rios 64
  Old Colonial 64
  Ole Jamaica 65
  Queva 65, **65**
  Riviera 65
  Solitaire 66, **66**
  Springtime **65, 66**
  Sundowner 56
  Surfside 66
  Tarantula **66**, 67
  Tea Punch 78
  Tropicana **66**, 67
  Zulu 67
Rye 11

Sabra 11
Saké 8, 11, 14, 16, **51**
Saké set 23
Sakini 54, **56**
Sally Anne 91
Salmon roe **37**
Salty Dog 28
Sambuca 11, 36
San Francisco **89**, 91
Sardi's, New York 6
Sazerack 56
Serving cocktails 36

Shaking 32
Shamrock 56
Shanghai Gin Fizz 56
Shenley Lodge 91, **92**
Sherry 11
Sherry glass 26, **27**
Shot glass **23**, 27
Sidecar 42
Silk Stockings 66
Singapore Sling 14, **16**
Sixty-Six 56
Skyline 56, **57**
Sloe gin 11
Smoked salmon rolls **37**
Sodastream 23
Solitaire 66, **66**
Somerset 78, **79**
Sours 42
Southern Comfort 11
Spirit-based Cocktails 44-57
Spirit Cocktail Glass 26, **27**
Spoons 23
Springtime 65, 66
Stinger 42, **43**
Stirring rod 27
Stocking up 14-17
Storing cocktails 36-37, 68
'Straight up' 36
Straining 32
Strawberry Fields 78, **79**
St. Charles 78
Sundowner 56
Surfside 66
Swizzle Stick **81**

Tamagozake 56
Tankard glass 26
Tantalize 56, **57**
Tarantula **66**, 67
Taronga Twist 78
Tea Punch 78
Temperance 92
Temptation 56
Tequila 11
Tequila Sunrise **66**, 67
The General 78, **79**
Tia Maria 11, 14
Toasted Almond 7, **7**
Triple Sec 11, 14
Tropicana **66**, 67
Tropic of Capricorn 67
'Twist' 36
Twister 79

Ugly Bug 92, **92**

Vanderbilt 57, **57**
Velvet Hammer 72
Vermouth 11, 14
Vesuvius 67

V.I.P. **66**, 67
Vodka 11, 14, **17**, 44
Vodka-based Cocktails
  Barbara 68
  Bloody Mary 43, **43**
  Bullshot 43
  Collins 42
  Green Widow **48**, 50
  Harvey Wallbanger 35, 50, **51**
  Hong Kong Fizz 50
  Katinka 51
  Marijka 52, **52**
  Moscow Melon 53, **54**
  Moscow Mule 53, **54**
  Off the Rails 53
  Zedd **66**, 67
Vodkatina 40

Waabine Cooler 92
Waiter's Friend 16, **21**
Washington 57
Wedding Bells 57
Whiskey, Irish 11
Whisk(e)y 11, 14, **17**, 44
Whisk(e)y-based Cocktails
  Benedict Arnold 46
  Blenheim 76
  Brooklyn 47, **47**
  Canada 47
  Colonial Boy 47, **49**
  Embassy Royale 50
  Hair of the Dog 94, **94**
  Hannibal Palace 62, **62**
  Kojak **62**, 63
  Lark 51
  Lulu 77, **79**
  Manhattan 40, 44
  Midori Sour 53, **53**
  Millionaire 53
  Mint Julep 32, **52**, 53
  Pennsylvania 78
  Pink Almond 54
  Royale 54, 55
  Sazerack 56
  Shamrock 56
  Sours 42
  Temptation 56
  Twister 79
Widow's Dream 72, **73**
Wine glasses 26
Wine goblet 27
Wine Cocktails 74-79

Yellow Dwarf 92, **92**

Zanzibar, London 9
Zanzibar Mai Tai 9, **9**
Zedd , 67, **67**
Zibi 92, **92**
Zulu 67

ACKNOWLEDGEMENTS

The publishers would like to thank the following individuals and companies for their kind assistance in supplying items for the photography in this book:

Cocktail equipment and glasses: The Cocktail Shop, Neal St, London W1 and 5 Avery Row, London W1; Heals, 196 Tottenham Court Road, London W1; Chinacraft Ltd, London.
Champagne and accessories: Michael Druitt, 9 Deanery Street, London W1.
Drinks: in particular the publishers would like to thank Matthew Clark & Sons Ltd, 183 Central Street, London EC1, who are distributors of De Kuyper Liqueurs in the U.K.; also Martini and Rossi Ltd, 80 Haymarket, London SW1; Pimm's Ltd, 63 Pall Mall, London SW1; Kenneth Abbott, 7 Cork Street, London W1. J. B. Reynier Ltd, London SW1 supplied the syrups.
Cover model: Amber, at Gavin Robinson, 30 Old Bond Street, London SW1.